JONAH
A MODERN COMMENTARY

LEONARD S. KRAVITZ
and
KERRY M. OLITZKY

URJ PRESS
NEW YORK, NEW YORK

For permission to reprint, please contact the URJ Press at:

URJ Press
633 Third Avenue
New York, NY 10017–6778

(212) 650–4124
press@urj.org

Library of Congress Cataloging-in-Publication Data

Kravitz, Leonard S.
   Jonah : a modern commentary / Leonard S. Kravitz and Kerry M. Olitzky.
     p. cm.
   Includes bibliographical references.
   ISBN-13: 978-0-8074-0860-5 (alk. paper)
   ISBN-10: 0-8074-0860-3 (alk. paper)
 1. Bible. O.T. Jonah—Commentaries. I. Olitzky, Kerry M. II. Title.
   BS1605.53.K73 2006
   224'.92077–dc22

                                                       200601499

Typesetting: El Ot Pre Press & Computing Ltd., Tel Aviv
This book is printed on acid-free paper.
Copyright © 2006 by URJ Press
Manufactured in the United States of America
10 9 8 7 6 5 4 3 2 1

Contents

Permissions

Acknowledgments

Who would have thought when we began teaching together nearly twenty years ago—in classrooms often next door to each other—that our collaboration would take the shape of the translating, commenting on, and editing of an ongoing series of sacred texts for the URJ Press, the Reform Movement, and the Jewish community at large? Our commitment to providing accessible texts for people so that they may fully claim them as their own has remained part of the bond we share even as our life's journeys have taken us to different places. For this privilege, we are grateful to many people.

We must thank Rabbi Hara Person—once our student, now a cherished colleague—for guiding us. She has done a superb job of painstakingly editing each volume and is definitely the silent partner in this series of sacred texts. We thank our many friends at the URJ Press, including Victor Ney, Zack Kolstein, Ron Ghatan, Lauren Dubin, Elizabeth Gutterman, and Debra Hirsch Corman, and on the staff of the Union for Reform Judaism itself for its continuous support and confidence in us. We thank Rabbi Eric Yoffie for providing the URJ with profound guidance and helping to nurture a renewed interest in and enthusiasm for the study of sacred literature. And we express our gratitude to Rabbi David Ellenson for offering a new vision for the students, faculty, and graduates of Hebrew Union College–Jewish Institute of Religion.

We also thank the many students who have given us the privilege to share our love of sacred text with them, including those at the Center for Religious Inquiry, St. Bartholomew's Church in New York City. This experiment, under the direction of our colleague Rabbi Leonard Schoolman, provides a bright light in the darkness in the lives of everyday people that threatens to separate us.

In addition, I, Kerry, thank my family—my wife, Sheryl; our boys, Avi and Jesse; and the newest member of our family, Sarah—who understand the circuitous path in life that I continue to follow and support me each step along the way. They know, as I do, that sharing of the words of Torah brings with it a profound spirit of renewal that is life-sustaining.

Leonard S. Kravitz
Kerry ("Shia") Olitzky
Sukkot 5767

Introduction

The Book of Jonah is well-known among Jews because it is read aloud on Yom Kippur afternoon, following the Torah reading during the *Minchah* service. The book itself is the fifth of twelve short prophetic works classically referred to as the Minor Prophets. However, the entire Book of Jonah, only four short chapters in length, contains only one prophecy. The entire length of that prophecy, contained in verse 3:4, is only five words. The rest of the book is the story of Jonah son of Amittai, a name that is clearly a pun on the Hebrew word for "truth." And even though we read it each year and know the details and its outcomes, it still continues to capture our attention anew because it is a good story.

While it is not entirely clear why the Book of Jonah was included in the Bible, particularly in the collection of prophetic texts, it might have been as a result of a reference to a man of that name in the time of Jeroboam (as noted in II Kings 14:25). The Jonah mentioned there correctly predicted that Jeroboam, king of Israel (784–748 B.C.E.), would win back land previously lost to the Assyrians. However, linguistic and historical markers lead scholars to place the text of the Book of Jonah much later. The influence of Aramaic on the Hebrew argues for a period after the Babylonian Exile (586–538 B.C.E.). For example, the term "king of Nineveh" (3:6) would not have been used while the Assyrian Empire still existed. The book may even date from as late as the third century B.C.E., based on the mention of a man named Jonah in a text by Ben Sira. But it was certainly the theme of the Book of Jonah rather than the identity of the prophet himself that seems to have caught the attention of canonizers, because it is the story of a man who was supposed to bring the word of God to the people of Nineveh. Nineveh was a major city in Assyria, a sworn enemy of Israel. Jonah had no desire to save its people. This city was located where Mosul, Iraq, is located today. Its leadership in the time of Jonah was no more friendly to Israel than its current leadership. Other prophets preached to the people of Israel. They did not want to be prophets because they were fearful that God would punish those who did not repent. Jonah did not want to become a prophet because he was afraid that the people would repent and still be punished. While Moses and Jeremiah considered themselves unworthy of the gift of prophecy, Jonah accepted the mantle but ran away from carrying through on the responsibility. Thus, even if his prophecy was limited and somewhat untraditional, his connection to God and function as a divine spokesperson certainly were not.

The Rabbis quickly run to Jonah's defense as a way of explaining away his strange behavior. They argue that he was afraid that if the people of Nineveh were to repent—as they indeed did—a comparison would be made between the stubbornness of the Jewish people and others, like those of Nineveh, who responded to God's call to repentance.

There might be another motivation for the author to colorfully paint the prophet as irascible and unpleasant. Perhaps Jonah reflects the author's reactions to the self-righteousness that he saw in other prophets. This author was not alone in seeing the prophets in such unbecoming light. Others felt the same way. The midrash (*Tanchuma, Vayishlach* 2), for example, tells us that God responded to these words of Isaiah —"I am a person of unclean lips and I dwell among a people of unclean lips" (Isaiah 6:5)—with the statement, "You can say that about yourself if you want, but you cannot say that about a people who recites the *Sh'ma* twice a day [as part of the daily liturgy]." The writer of this midrash continues by adding to God's words, "Smash the mouth of the one who speaks evil of My children."

As is the case in many sections of sacred literature, the biblical Jonah is far different from the Jonah that is created in the minds of the Rabbis. And among those Rabbis, there is further disagreement. To gain some insight into these differences and add historical perspective to our own comments, we will take an in-depth look at four interpreters, beginning with the *Targum*, the Aramaic translation of the text from the third century of the Common Era in the Land of Israel, which is as much commentary as translation. The *Targum* is written in Aramaic because that was the language that was spoken by Jews at the time. Writing in Aramaic would have been equivalent to translating the text into English today. Because the goal of the translator was to make the text accessible to the reader, the *Targum* added information and guidance to the translation, thereby transforming it into a commentary. These additions were meant to aid the reader to become a better Jew and a better person. It was written for the everyday person who had come to hear the text read aloud in public assembly and thus was meant to function much like today's *d'var Torah* offered by contemporary rabbis and teachers. Its insights remain relevant today because in reading its translation—and additions—we get a sense of what was important to Jewish everyday living as seen through the prism of Jonah.

We will also consider the comprehensive commentary of Rabbi Solomon ben Isaac, better known as Rashi (1040–1105 C.E.). Next we will see what Abraham ibn Ezra (1098–1164 C.E.) has to say about the text from the perspective of one who was born in Spain; lived in Mantua, Rome, and London; and was the model for Robert Browning's poem "Rabbi Ben Ezra." Finally, we will review the commentary of Rabbi David Kimchi (1160–1235 C.E.), who lived in Narbonne, France, and was known by the acronym Radak (often spelled Redak). His commentary is a creative blend of midrash and philosophy.

As a prophetic work, the Book of Jonah parallels the stories of Elijah, Jeremiah, and Joel. Unlike many of the other books of the Bible, most scholars consider the book as one literary entity. However, some will note the possibility of additional texts throughout the book (such as 4:5). Others claim that these are not additions, but rather, they reflect the literary style of the author, who describes the religious significance of events after the action before continuing the story. Even Jonah's well-known psalm (2:3–10)—spoken from the belly of the fish—doesn't seem to fit the context. Yet its language reflects the language used through the book. Perhaps it originally came from a different source but was always part of the original composition of the book.

Nevertheless, there appear to be some internal inconsistencies in the text that require explanation. For example, why did the king order the people to put on sackcloth and to fast when they were already doing so on their own (3:5–8)? Additionally, why did Jonah have to sit in the shade of the plant when he was already sitting in the shade of a booth (4:5–6)? These are just a few of the questions that the commentary will address.

Perhaps most appealing about Jonah for the canonizers of the Bible is the theme of repentance that colors the entire book. According to the Talmud, the Book of Jonah is to be read on Yom Kippur afternoon, during the *Minchah* service. What is unclear, however, is whether the requirement was made as a result of the book's prominence or whether this mandate contributed to the book's religious and literary fame. God sends the reluctant Jonah to tell the citizens of Nineveh that if they don't change their ways, they are doomed. While it is implicit that God will destroy the city, the message is that those who practice the ways of Nineveh are doomed by their own behaviors irrespective of God's meting out of punishment. The entire city repents. This teaches the reader that spiritual renewal—real change—is possible. It also teaches us on Yom Kippur not to run away from our own wrongdoing. Furthermore, we learn from the experience that entire communities do not have to bear the burden of a sinful legacy, as is the case with Germany. After all, the government of the modern state of Israel has embraced modern Germany irrespective of the role of its former leaders in the Holocaust. Although Jonah is disappointed that God relents, the lesson of divine forgiveness and mercy informs the remainder of the text. The author also characterizes the need for human acceptance of the divine role in the world and in the process of repentance. God wants people to turn to life. And just like the people in Nineveh, the people gathered in the synagogue for Yom Kippur—which is drawing to a close by the time Jonah is read—feel like they are going to make it. Jonah is every man and every woman sitting in the synagogue on Yom Kippur, facing life and our responsibilities to others as we try to navigate a righteous path in the world.

CHAPTER ONE

א:א וַיְהִי דְּבַר־יְהֹוָה אֶל־יוֹנָה בֶן־אֲמִתַּי לֵאמֹר:

1:1 NOW THE WORD OF *ADONAI* CAME TO JONAH SON OF
AMITTAI:

This verse sets up the entire book that follows and lays out Jonah's prophetic mission.
We know next to nothing about Jonah. Yet the very first sentence of the book
indicates that God communicates with him. But how does God communicate with
Jonah? In its translation, the *Targum* always avoids appearing to promote anthropomorphism, so it specifies that "the word of prophecy" came from God. This minor
distinction creates distance between God and the process of prophecy by suggesting
"the word came from before God," rather than "from God." This question of how
we communicate with God becomes particularly important as we approach Yom
Kippur. How do we ask God for forgiveness, and how does God tell us that we have
been forgiven?

Ibn Ezra begins his commentary by identifying this Jonah with his namesake in the
Book of Kings. Nevertheless, he asks the same fundamental question about this book:
how could anyone who is aware of God's work in the world think that it is possible to
run from God's presence, let alone rebel against the divine request to prophesy?

Although he quotes Saadyah Gaon, who suggests that Jonah's flight to Tarshish follows a second visit to Nineveh, Ibn Ezra rejects such an assertion. It is possible that
Saadyah may be referring to the accounts of Jonah as told in *Pirkei D'Rabbi Eliezer*,
chapter 10, and in the beginning of *Midrash Yonah*; these two midrashim explain that
Jonah flees because this mission to Nineveh is the third on which he has been sent.
The first one is described in II Kings 14:25; as noted in the introduction to this
volume, Jonah's predictions are fulfilled. According to Saadyah, although he provides
no biblical support for such an assertion, the second mission sends the prophet to
Jerusalem. As far as Jonah is concerned, that mission has mixed results. He prophesies

1

destruction, but the people repent and are saved. As a result, the people call Jonah a "false prophet." God then sends Jonah to Nineveh as his third prophetic assignment. The midrash imagines Jonah thinking to himself, "If I prophesy destruction once again and the people repent and are saved, they too will call me a false prophet. It is bad enough to be called a false prophet by Jews. In this case, I will be called a false prophet by non-Jews." So he flees to Tarshish. It appears that he is concerned about his reputation, an ultimately shallow consideration that provides an important lesson at Yom Kippur on caring for others versus caring for oneself. An alternate reading would be that he is merely unwilling to save Israel's enemies.

Ibn Ezra continues his comment by citing a Rabbinic adage found in the *M'chilta* (*Bo*, chapter 1): Jonah insists on focusing on the honor of the child (Israel) and does not insist on the honor of the parent (God). Ibn Ezra further notes that even Moses resists his prophetic call. He tries to explain the difference between Moses and Jonah in this way: Some people by their very nature can write poetry, while others require training. Those who need training sometimes can write, but often they are unable to do so. All the other prophets—except for Moses—receive their prophecy through visions and dreams. [Here Ibn Ezra anticipates a notion that Maimonides explicates in his *Guide for the Perplexed* 2:34, 36, 45.] Jonah flees *milifnei Adonai* (from the presence of God). In other words, Jonah doesn't really flee *from* God. Rather, it is only in the context of a dream or through a vision that he is fleeing. The commentator is teaching a theological lesson: there is no place where one can be away from God. On Yom Kippur the lesson is especially poignant. We admit to our sins although God is already fully aware of them. The process is thus about cleansing ourselves rather than informing God. As we own up to our shortcomings, we renew ourselves for the new year and are able to begin again in a new relationship to God.

While Redak calls the reader's attention to the same Rabbinic statement that Ibn Ezra quotes regarding the concern for a child over the parent, he takes this opportunity to ask why the Book of Jonah was included in the Bible at all. He reminds us that the text deals with a city that is not in the Land of Israel. It does not deal with the Jewish people. There is no mention whatsoever of Israel—land or people. So Redak reasons that the book contains a moral lesson for the people. If a foreign people are so ready and willing to repent, so much so that they repent after the prophet's first communication with them, shouldn't the people of Israel—whose prophets speak to them all the time—start the process toward repentance? In Redak's reading, this group of "others" serves as a model of the behavior we are supposed to be taking on in the first place.

א:ב קוּם לֵךְ אֶל־נִינְוֵה הָעִיר הַגְּדוֹלָה וּקְרָא עָלֶיהָ כִּי־עָלְתָה רָעָתָם לְפָנָי:

1:2 "GET UP AND GO TO THE GREAT CITY OF NINEVEH,
AND ANNOUNCE THERE THAT THEIR EVIL HAS COME
UP TO ME."

God's message is quite clear. The people of Nineveh have gone astray, and God sends Jonah to deliver the message of repentance. It seems that this is the message of the Yom Kippur liturgy as well. The implication of the message is that God has taken notice and the people had better change their ways or prepare themselves for a divine response to their behaviors.

How does God communicate with Jonah about fulfilling his task? The *Targum* understands *uk'ra* (literally, "and call") as "and prophesy," which we have translated as "announce." For Rashi, who takes the word more literally, "and call" becomes "My call"—that which I would have you call. Redak considers *uk'ra* as more than "call, proclaim, or announce" to the people of Nineveh that God has become aware of their evil. Instead, he suggests it means that Jonah is to tell them what their evildoings will result in. The people don't care about how Jonah does it. They only want to know the end result. While this outcome is not stated this early in the text, Ibn Ezra deduces the message from verse 3:4, which indicates that Nineveh will be overthrown. He explains that Nineveh is the royal city of Assyria, which had been destroyed. Ibn Ezra offers an additional insight: God exercises divine providence over the nations when there is evil and violence, as evidenced in what God did to the generation of the Flood and to the people of Sodom. He states this also as a warning to those listening to the text being read. Although those observing Yom Kippur may not consider their sins to be as grave as those of Sodom, Ibn Ezra implies that there is a "slippery slope" for such behavior. In pointing out what could happen, he is trying to persuade people to repent, irrespective of the severity or relative insignificance of their sins. Since violence disrupts the kind of civilization desired by God, God expresses concern for all nations, although God is only concerned with the specific nature of the transgressions in relationship to Israel.

א:ג וַיָּקָם יוֹנָה לִבְרֹחַ תַּרְשִׁישָׁה מִלִּפְנֵי יְהֹוָה וַיֵּרֶד יָפוֹ וַיִּמְצָא אֳנִיָּה בָּאָה תַרְשִׁישׁ וַיִּתֵּן שְׂכָרָהּ וַיֵּרֶד בָּהּ לָבוֹא עִמָּהֶם תַּרְשִׁישָׁה מִלִּפְנֵי יְהֹוָה:

1:3 BUT JONAH GOT UP TO FLEE TO TARSHISH TO AVOID OBEYING *ADONAI*. HE WENT DOWN TO JAFFA, FOUND A BOAT GOING TO TARSHISH, PAID THE FARE, AND WENT DOWN SO HE COULD GO WITH THOSE ABOARD TO TARSHISH AND THUS AVOID OBEYING *ADONAI*.

Perhaps we might respond as does Jonah—running away from God's directive and our responsibility to it. The text is geographically specific, mentioning Jaffa, on the coast of Israel. It is not uncommon for someone to try to literally flee the country to escape punishment or responsibility. Yet read in the context of Yom Kippur, the verse can also be understood as a metaphor for the ways in which some avoid owning up to their wrongdoings and avoid the strenuous spiritual work of repentance.

As in its commentary on 1:1, in a continuing effort to avoid any anthropomorphism, the *Targum* explains *milifnei Adonai* (literally, "from the face of God"), translated here as "obeying *Adonai*," as "from prophesying in the name of God."

According to Rashi, Jonah's flight to Tarshish is due to his mistaken view that the Divine Presence of God does not dwell outside the Land of Israel. This is a theme we see in other places in the Bible, too. Admittedly, while many today feel a special connection to God when visiting or living in Israel, few would say that God's presence resides only there. Rashi reminds us in the form of a parable that there are many people whom God could enlist to bring Jonah back. Bringing to the reader's attention a notion that emerges frequently throughout Rabbinic literature in defense of Jonah, Rashi emphasizes that Jonah's flight is intended to save those among the people of Israel who are unwilling to repent to avoid being condemned, in contrast to the people of Nineveh, who are eager to repent. He further notes that Jonah is so eager to get to Tarshish that he pays the fare upon entering the boat rather than when he disembarks, which apparently was the usual practice. Rashi wants to communicate to the reader, as the rabbi does on Yom Kippur to those gathered in prayer, that one can always repent—even if you are not prepared to do so now.

אːד וַיהוָה הֵטִיל רוּחַ־גְּדוֹלָה אֶל־הַיָּם וַיְהִי סַעַר־גָּדוֹל בַּיָּם וְהָאֳנִיָּה חִשְּׁבָה לְהִשָּׁבֵר:

1:4 BUT *ADONAI* SENT A STRONG WIND UPON THE SEA
SO THAT THERE WAS A GREAT STORM ON THE SEA, SO
THAT THE BOAT WAS ABOUT TO BREAK APART.

Adonai—the specifically named God of Israel, the God of the Jewish people—intervenes and is responsible for sending forth the wind that threatens the vessel, apparently as a direct response to Jonah's action. The use of God's specific name connected to the people of Israel foretells the recognition of Jonah's God by the sailors. According to the narrative, it is part of God's plan not to let Jonah run away from his task. The text serves to remind us that on Yom Kippur it is not possible to run from God and we need to face up to our actions. This verse also touches on the issue of free will, in highlighting the tension between Jonah's disobedience toward God and God maneuvering a situation in which Jonah becomes willing to make the choice to obey.

In the Hebrew, this verse contains an unusual use of the root *ch-sh-v* in the intensive form (called the *pi-eil* form). As is indicated in the Koehler-Baumgartner's *The Hebrew and Aramaic Lexicon of the Old Testament* (p. 360), the root—and the form in which it is used—generally has the meaning of "request." In this context, the word is used to indicate that something is about to happen. The authors of the *Lexicon* refer readers of Jonah to Daniel 2:13, where the parallel Aramaic root of *b-a-a* is used to mean that something is about to occur, although it, too, is generally used to mean "to request."

Ibn Ezra helps us to understand the use of *heitil* (literally, "cast" or "threw"). While we have translated it idiomatically in this verse as "sent," he suggests that it is used with regard to a wind that came from the direction of the land out to the sea. He claims that this kind of a wind is caused only when there is a river that empties out into the sea. Apparently, he learned this from the verse later in Jonah (2:4): "You threw me into the deep, into the heart of the seas. The *nahar* surrounded me." Just as the Koehler-Baumgartner *Lexicon* (p. 676) suggests, although *nahar* generally has the meaning of "river," in this case it means "sea currents."

Redak explains the problematic verb *chish'vah*. The members of the crew think that the boat is about to break up. They all seek to understand the source of the unusual wind that took them by surprise. The sailors interpret the actions as coming from a god, in this case the God of Israel.

א:ה וַיִּירְאוּ הַמַּלָּחִים וַיִּזְעֲקוּ אִישׁ אֶל־אֱלֹהָיו וַיָּטִלוּ אֶת־הַכֵּלִים אֲשֶׁר בָּאֳנִיָּה אֶל־הַיָּם לְהָקֵל מֵעֲלֵיהֶם וְיוֹנָה יָרַד אֶל־יַרְכְּתֵי הַסְּפִינָה וַיִּשְׁכַּב וַיֵּרָדַם:

1:5 THE FRIGHTENED SAILORS CRIED OUT EACH TO HIS OWN GOD. THEN, TO LIGHTEN THE LOAD, THEY THREW EVERYTHING OVERBOARD. JONAH, HOWEVER, WENT DOWN TO THE LOWEST PART OF THE SHIP AND LAY DOWN AND WENT TO SLEEP.

The author paints a word picture of panic, but in the midst of such a state, Jonah goes to the lowest point in the boat, where there is the least calm—running away once again—and is able to go to sleep. This action emphasizes Jonah's disregard for his fate. Since the sailors are throwing many things overboard, the author implies that the boat is not primarily a passenger vessel. Rather, it must be a merchant ship as well. The term in Hebrew to describe what is thrown over is simply *keilim*. This word could refer to different kinds of merchandise, including pots, pieces of equipment, baggage, utensils, and musical instruments. (See Koehler-Baumgartner, *Lexicon,* pp. 478–79.) The word is used in II Kings 4:3–6 to refer to oil flasks. These would have been easy to throw overboard and were commonly carried by merchant ships. While the Hebrew indicates that Jonah goes to the lowest part of the ship, it is difficult to determine the actual part that is indicated by *yark'tei has'finah.* Koehler-Baumgartner (p. 439) indicates that the first word generally means "rear" or "far part." Thus, the word might mean "stern." However, the author tells us that Jonah *yarad* (goes down, went down) to the *yark'tei has'finah,* which suggests that Jonah goes down into the ship, not merely in the direction of the stern, but as far away as he can go. The specificity of the location does not seem to matter to the author. Wherever it is exactly, he seems to go to a place where the sailors are not assembled. By doing so, Jonah may feel that he can avoid a confrontation with the sailors and thereby with his own path in life. The *Targum* understands Jonah to go down *l'arit shidah,* "to the lowest part of the box," that is, the lowest part of the interior of the ship. That is why we have translated the phrase as "the lowest part of the ship." But the *Targum* is not satisfied with simply translating the text. It adds the notion that the terrified sailors cry out to their pagan deities and "saw that they derived no benefit from them."

In Rashi's opinion, these particular sailors actually provide the manpower to move the ship in the water. He reminds us that their actions indicate that the crew is made up of people of various geographic and religious origins, but none are able to force the God of Israel to do anything to save the ship. Ibn Ezra takes the word for "sailors" (*malachim*) as a reference to the ship's officers. He even suggests that Jonah simply went to the *yark'tei* (one end of the boat) because he was seasick! After all, he thinks that Jonah has not entered the hold of the ship until that point. Adding his own perspective on the verse, Redak tells us that the *malachim* are actually the oarsmen.

א:ו וַיִּקְרַב אֵלָיו רַב הַחֹבֵל וַיֹּאמֶר לוֹ מַה־לְּךָ נִרְדָּם קוּם קְרָא אֶל־
אֱלֹהֶיךָ אוּלַי יִתְעַשֵּׁת הָאֱלֹהִים לָנוּ וְלֹא נֹאבֵד:

1:6 THE SHIP'S CAPTAIN CAME UP TO HIM AND SAID,
"WHAT'S WITH YOU, NOW TO BE SLEEPING? GET UP!
PRAY TO YOUR GOD. MAYBE THAT GOD WILL THINK OF
US SO THAT WE WON'T BE DESTROYED."

The ship's captain does not seem pleased with Jonah's nonchalant attitude and is concerned about the welfare of his ship and his crew. Unconcerned about the source of the divine intervention, he calls on Jonah to implore his god to intervene on behalf of the sailors. It is unusual that someone would call upon an adherent of a different god to solicit the intervention of that god, because doing so is to acknowledge the power of that god. The Hebrew word *yitasheit*, which comes from the root *ayin-shin-tav*, occurs only here. Our translation "think" follows Rashi and is derived from the context and from the same Aramaic root in Daniel 6:4. The Targum translates the word as *yitracheim* (will have pity), implying that the captain is asking Jonah's god to take pity on them. While Rashi derives its meaning from the same source as the *Targum*, he adds that it comes from *eshtonotav* (his thoughts), which is found in Psalm 146:4. He explains the captain's question as an understandable outburst: "Now is not the time to sleep!"

Ibn Ezra connects the title *rav hachoveil* (captain) with *chavalim* (ropes). Thus, it is the captain who tells the crew to pull the ropes that raise and lower the sails. While Redak makes a similar statement about the derivation of this word, he adds that *choveil* is a collective plural of *chov'lim* (sailors). The captain's call from the midst of the pages of the Book of Jonah is also a call to us to awake and get ourselves on the path of renewal and repentance. We have to be shaken, aroused, before we realize that we are close to a death of the soul.

א:ז וַיֹּאמְרוּ אִישׁ אֶל־רֵעֵהוּ לְכוּ וְנַפִּילָה גוֹרָלוֹת וְנֵדְעָה בְּשֶׁלְּמִי הָרָעָה הַזֹּאת לָנוּ וַיַּפִּלוּ גּוֹרָלוֹת וַיִּפֹּל הַגּוֹרָל עַל־יוֹנָה:

> 1:7 THE CREW MEMBERS SAID TO EACH OTHER, "LET'S CAST LOTS SO THAT WE CAN FIND OUT WHO IS THE CAUSE OF THE DISASTER THAT HAS FALLEN UPON US." THEY CAST LOTS AND IT FELL ON JONAH.

Apparently, this was a common form of divination in the ancient world. Rashi explains that they cast lots because they see other boats navigating the waters without any problem. Thus, they reason that their misfortune must be a direct result of someone on board their vessel. Like Rashi, many of the classical commentators point to *Pirkei D'Rabbi Eliezer* as the source for this explanation and offer no glosses of their own. The readers, of course, are not at all surprised when Jonah appears to be at fault. In our own lives we do not realize that we are the source of both our problems and the potential solution.

א:ח וַיֹּאמְרוּ אֵלָיו הַגִּידָה־נָּא לָנוּ בַּאֲשֶׁר לְמִי־הָרָעָה הַזֹּאת לָנוּ מַה־
מְלַאכְתְּךָ וּמֵאַיִן תָּבוֹא מָה אַרְצֶךָ וְאֵי־מִזֶּה עַם אָתָּה:

1:8 THEY SAID TO HIM, "YOU ARE THE ONE WHO
BROUGHT THIS DISASTER ON US. TELL US, WHAT'S
YOUR BUSINESS? WHERE ARE YOU FROM? WHAT'S YOUR
COUNTRY [OF ORIGIN]? AND WHAT IS YOUR PEOPLE
[OF ORIGIN]?"

Now that the crew has determined that Jonah is the source of their misfortune at sea, they want to discern the actual cause. In his comment on the verse, Rashi has the crew asking Jonah what sin he has committed. Is it related to his business? Or is their difficulty due to some evil decree that has been proclaimed against his people or his homeland? Perhaps it is a result of a sin committed by his people, rather than by Jonah himself.

Here Ibn Ezra disagrees with Rashi. If God had decreed that a specific place or person should be destroyed, then those in a different place would not be frightened, because they were not involved with that specific place or person. Moreover, most people make their living by means of a particular business. Since a person's livelihood usually indicates something about his life's situation, it makes no difference to travel to a different place. Ibn Ezra simply says that there are places where most people are good and these places would therefore protect even a sinner.

Redak expands on Rashi's line of questioning. He places specific questions in the mouths of the sailors. The sailors understand that Jonah has to have done something very wrong for God to threaten all their lives. Often people don't realize how their actions significantly impact the lives of others. According to Redak, the sailors want to know in what kind of deceitful violence Jonah was involved. Did he do something wrong where he lived? Are all the citizens of his country wicked, or just him? Now that blame is pointed at him, they are sure he must be guilty of something terrible.

א:ט וַיֹּאמֶר אֲלֵיהֶם עִבְרִי אָנֹכִי וְאֶת־יְהֹוָה אֱלֹהֵי הַשָּׁמַיִם אֲנִי יָרֵא
אֲשֶׁר־עָשָׂה אֶת־הַיָּם וְאֶת־הַיַּבָּשָׁה:

1:9 HE SAID TO THEM, "I AM A HEBREW, AND I REVERE
ADONAI, THE GOD OF HEAVEN WHO MADE THE SEA
AND THE DRY LAND."

Jews are known by different terms throughout history. Here the term "Hebrew" is used. In other times it will be "Israelites," and other times it will be "Jew." While this verse appears to be a response to a specific question, Jonah is also taking the opportunity to make a theological statement. This answer is also the way Jonah chooses to describe the Jewish people, offering an insight into the context that produced this book. In subsequent times, places, and texts, the Jewish people have been described in different ways. Jonah uses the term "Hebrew" as a means of distinguishing these people from others who live outside the Land of Israel. This is in contrast to how this term is used in other biblical sources. Although living in Canaan, Abraham (then called Abram) is the first to be called a Hebrew (Genesis 14:13). In Egypt, Joseph is called a Hebrew (Genesis 39:14, 41:12), as are the women tended by the midwives (Exodus 1:16, 1:19). Similarly, the man Moses sees being beaten by an Egyptian is called a Hebrew (Exodus 2:11). Here, alone at sea, Jonah calls himself a Hebrew, connecting himself to a particular people and set of beliefs. As a reflection of its own time and place, the *Targum* translates *ivri* (Hebrew) as *y'hudaah* (Jew).

Ibn Ezra makes note of the order in which Jonah answers the questions put to him, responding first to the last question. He tells the crew that he is a descendant of Eber (Genesis 10:21) and that he fears no one except *Adonai*, from whose charge he has fled, knowing full well that God is the Master of all. For Ibn Ezra, this is Judaism's core belief, just as it becomes the prism through which we see all else when we consider our lives and our relationship with God, the Sovereign of all.

Redak suggests to us that Jonah does not answer the crew's question about the nature of his business (as a prophet) because he does not want to lie to them. He mentions that God is responsible for the land and the sea to intimate that God was indeed responsible for the storm that they are experiencing. The inclusion of the word "heaven" indicates that God is in control of everything.

It is clear that this book, as reflected in this verse and the comments on it, is as much theology as it is parable. Similarly, Yom Kippur more than any other holiday on the calendar makes a major theological statement: God is the Source of all.

אי וַיִּֽירְא֤וּ הָֽאֲנָשִׁים֙ יִרְאָ֣ה גְדוֹלָ֔ה וַיֹּאמְר֥וּ אֵלָ֖יו מַה־זֹּ֣את עָשִׂ֑יתָ כִּֽי־ יָדְע֣וּ הָֽאֲנָשִׁ֗ים כִּֽי־מִלִּפְנֵ֤י יְהוָה֙ ה֣וּא בֹרֵ֔חַ כִּ֥י הִגִּ֖יד לָהֶֽם׃

1:10 THE MEMBERS OF THE CREW WERE EXTREMELY FRIGHT-ENED, AND THEY SAID TO HIM, "WHAT HAVE YOU DONE?" WHEN THEY FOUND OUT—SINCE HE TOLD THEM THAT HE WAS RUNNING AWAY FROM *ADONAI*—

The second part of this must be read in connection with the verse that follows. While it is only a result of the way the verses are numbered, reading one verse at a time adds a dramatic element to the retelling of the story.

While Rashi continues the question "What have you done?" with the phrase "to run away from such a Ruler," emphasizing God's omnipresence and the absurdity of Jonah's action, Ibn Ezra sees some wordplay taking place in the verse. Jonah says, *Ani yarei*, "I revere" (literally, "I fear"), and the sailors' response is *vayir'u* (they feared), translated as "were extremely frightened." For Ibn Ezra, the question "What have you done?" is more of an exclamation than a statement and follows Jonah's explanation that he is running away from God.

Redak wants to fill in the details of the entire discussion between Jonah and the sailors and leave little to the imagination of the reader. When Jonah tells the crew that he reveres the God of the heavens, Redak supplies their response: "If that is so, why is there is a storm?" He replies, "I am a prophet, and *Adonai* has sent me to Nineveh. Not wanting to go there, I left Israel, which is the land of prophecy." Redak thus imagines Jonah making a point about his mission that is absent in the plain reading of the text, attributing a greater sense of self-awareness to Jonah. And it is self-awareness that is an indispensable part of the *t'shuvah* process on Yom Kippur. Who we are is made more clear in presence of the Divine, as we stand naked before God on Yom Kippur.

אːיא וַיֹּאמְרוּ אֵלָיו מַה־נַּעֲשֶׂה לָּךְ וְיִשְׁתֹּק הַיָּם מֵעָלֵינוּ כִּי הַיָּם הוֹלֵךְ וְסֹעֵר:

1:11 They said to him, "What do we have to do to you to quiet the sea?" Because the storm was getting worse and worse.

This part of the ongoing dialogue between the crew and Jonah leads to a dramatic denouement in the story. The crew is clearly running out of options. Ibn Ezra interprets this as the crew asking Jonah for advice. Apparently, their own prayers have not worked and they are getting desperate. According to Redak's understanding of the verse, there is no hope for the storm to abate since it seems to be intensifying. He explains that the word *v'yishtok* (quiet) is derived from the sound of waves. On Yom Kippur, we are like the sailor. We plead to God, thinking what we can do to save ourselves. The sailor speaks of a bodily death, whereas Yom Kippur is about the death of our souls as much as it is about the death of our bodies.

אːיב וַיֹּאמֶר אֲלֵיהֶם שָׂאוּנִי וַהֲטִילֻנִי אֶל־הַיָּם וְיִשְׁתֹּק הַיָּם מֵעֲלֵיכֶם כִּי יוֹדֵעַ אָנִי כִּי בְשֶׁלִּי הַסַּעַר הַגָּדוֹל הַזֶּה עֲלֵיכֶם:

1:12 He said to them, "Pick me up and throw me into the sea. The sea will become quiet, for I know that it is because of me that this terrible storm has come upon you."

The drama continues to build, and again the commentators read this verse in a straightforward manner. Ibn Ezra reads this as an expression of Jonah's desire to die so as to prevent the people of Nineveh from repenting. He adds that Jonah would not have made the offer had he not previously heard that they were willing to cast him overboard. For Redak, Jonah's offer is a confession of his own sin.

א:יג וַיַּחְתְּרוּ הָאֲנָשִׁים לְהָשִׁיב אֶל־הַיַּבָּשָׁה וְלֹא יָכֹלוּ כִּי הַיָּם הוֹלֵךְ
וְסֹעֵר עֲלֵיהֶם:

1:13 THE CREW TRIED HARD TO ROW TO SHORE BUT WERE
UNABLE TO DO SO BECAUSE THE STORM AT SEA
INTENSIFIED.

The root *ch-t-r* generally has the meaning of "dig," as in Exodus 22:1 and Ezekiel 8:8,
but here it has the meaning of "row." Perhaps its use is descriptive of oarsmen digging
their oars into the water, that is, rowing, or trying hard, "digging in" to stay alive.
Similarly, the verb *shay'tin*, used by the *Targum* to translate *vayacht'ru* (they rowed),
usually has the meaning of "swim," another word that implies a sense of trying to
survive.

   Rashi picks up the other meaning in his suggestion that the crew members are
exerting themselves in their rowing just as an individual does when digging through a
wall, emphasizing the difficulty or even desperation of their task. In a similar comment, Ibn Ezra explains that the members of the crew look like they are digging as
they row. For those who take the work of Yom Kippur seriously, it is similarly hard. We
have to work hard to survive, to repent, to be renewed. We are desperate for another
chance to do differently, to do better in the new year ahead.

א:יד וַיִּקְרְאוּ אֶל־יְהוָֹה וַיֹּאמְרוּ אָנָּה יְהוָֹה אַל־נָא נֹאבְדָה בְּנֶפֶשׁ הָאִישׁ
הַזֶּה וְאַל־תִּתֵּן עָלֵינוּ דָּם נָקִיא כִּי־אַתָּה יְהוָֹה כַּאֲשֶׁר חָפַצְתָּ
עָשִׂיתָ:

1:14 THEY CRIED OUT TO *ADONAI* [IN PANIC], "O GOD,
PLEASE DON'T LET US PERISH BECAUSE OF THIS MAN'S
LIFE NOR MAKE US SHED INNOCENT BLOOD! YOU ARE
ADONAI. YOU CAN DO WHATEVER YOU WANT."

Some people come to the synagogue on Yom Kippur because they understand the
process of repentance and the importance of a relationship with God in our lives.
Others are persuaded to do so by life-changing experiences. The sailors have come to

recognize God's role in the universe through their powerlessness in this situation. The crew members directly call out to *Adonai*. They do not address their own deities. This episode at sea is a process of transformation for the crew, whereas Jonah will still need additional time and experiences before he can undergo a real transformation.

We have translated *v'al titein aleinu dam naki* (literally, "don't place innocent blood upon us") as "nor make us shed innocent blood." This phrase shows that the crew members have a conscience. Though they are not followers of *Adonai*, they have a moral code.

The *Targum* translates "they cried out" as *v'tzaliu* (and they prayed) and explains "this man's *nefesh* [soul, life]" as *b'chovat* (by the sin of), that is, "by the sin of this man's life/soul." The *Targum* also avoids any possibility of anthropomorphism by translating "whatever You want" as *k'ma d'raava* (as is Your will). For Rashi, the word *nefesh* (soul) is a reference to the sin of harming Jonah. Ibn Ezra reads the statement that "they cried" to mean that by this point the sailors all believe in God and in the power of repentance and are calling out to God. This final statement in the verse is for him an affirmation that the storm was indeed caused by the Divine. That is also the case with Yom Kippur. Over the course of twenty-five hours, we recognize God as the Source of our lives, even if we are predisposed to such a belief. The reading of Jonah late in the day helps to underline this process of acknowledging God as we return to God.

אָ:טו וַיִּשְׂאוּ אֶת־יוֹנָה וַיְטִלֻהוּ אֶל־הַיָּם וַיַּעֲמֹד הַיָּם מִזַּעְפּוֹ:

1:15 THEY PICKED JONAH UP AND THREW HIM INTO THE SEA. AND THE SEA STOPPED ITS RAGING.

While it would seem that Jonah's suggestion has worked, it is not clear why the sea should be settled and the storm subside just because Jonah is thrown into it. The calming of the storm does serve to confirm for the crew their new acknowledgment of God's power. It also reminds Jonah that ultimately he can't outsmart God, as it reminds us of this as well. The power of God, even in this case to stir up or calm the sea, is greater than anything we humans are capable of.

Ibn Ezra tells us that the verse uses the root *z-a-f* (raging) as a metaphor, as it is used in Genesis 40:6 to mean "disturbed."

14

א:טז וַיִּירְאוּ הָאֲנָשִׁים יִרְאָה גְדוֹלָה אֶת־יְהֹוָה וַיִּזְבְּחוּ־זֶבַח לַיהֹוָה וַיִּדְּרוּ
נְדָרִים:

1:16 THE CREW MEMBERS WERE EXTREMELY AFRAID OF
ADONAI, SO THEY OFFERED A SACRIFICE TO *ADONAI*
AND MADE VOWS.

While the expression "fear of *Adonai*" is a statement of reverence when it appears in
the Bible, here the meaning is somewhat different. The fact that the author uses the
phrase *vayir'u haanashim yirah g'dolah et Adonai* (literally, "the men feared God, a
great fear") suggests that the author meant that the relation of the pagan sailors to the
Deity is based on actual fear rather than reverence. On Yom Kippur, fear and reverence are also mixed, and it is often difficult to discern one from the other. And the
fear—of death—is real. That is what brings some to synagogue on Yom Kippur.

In its translation of the verse, the *Targum* adds the word *va'amaru* (they said or
thought) before *l'dabacha* (to sacrifice). This gives the sense that the crew are thinking
of sacrificing at a later time, since they cannot perform sacrifices on the boat.

Rashi explains that the vows the sailors make are part of the conversion process,
but Redak suggests that the sailors vow to give charity to the poor. Like so many in our
midst today, they simply cast their lot with the followers of the God of Israel and
follow in their ways, choosing the path of least resistance.

False Prophet

While prophets were spokespersons for God, prophetic speech and behaviors could
be imitated by anyone. Thus, the challenge faced by the ancient Israelites was how to
determine between prophets—those appointed by God—and false prophets who sought
to mislead the people. Since the Bible recognized the existence of other prophets and
their ability to perform "miracles," the only test for real prophecy was that the prophecy
of true prophets came true. This criterion raises an additional question: how long does
one wait for a prophecy to come to fruition in order to affirm the prophetic role of its
visionary? Moreover, God could change the plans communicated to a prophet—as is the

case in the story of Jonah. Furthermore, for Israel, the words of the prophets were as much words of instruction as they were insights into the future. Jeremiah suggests that the true prophet is the one who is willing to make entreaty to God on behalf of the people (Jeremiah 27:18). This is particularly the case when the prophet is predicting doom for the people. The true prophet is willing to risk his reputation in order to save the people. While many of the criteria for determining true prophecy were determined by Jeremiah, they were codified by Maimonides in *Y'sodei HaTorah*, chapters 8–10.

Repentance

While repentance (*t'shuvah*) is usually associated with the Ten Days of Repentance that begin on Rosh HaShanah and end on Yom Kippur, *t'shuvah* (literally, "returning to God") is an act Jews should undertake throughout their lives. According to Jewish tradition, it is a prerequisite for divine forgiveness. If one does not repent, divine pardon, which is always waiting, will not be proffered. Rabbi Eliezer said, "Repent one day before your death. Since no one knows when death will come, spend all your days in repentance" (Babylonian Talmud, *Shabbat* 153a).

Saadyah Gaon

Saadyah ben Joseph (882–942), from Fayyum, Egypt, is considered by most to be the father of medieval Jewish philosophy. He was the first to develop the notions of Islamic theology and philosophy in an independent manner. Similarly, he was the first to develop a philosophical justification for Judaism. He received his training in Egypt, where he lived the first thirty years of his life. He subsequently lived in the Land of Israel, Syria, and Babylonia. In 928, he became the *gaon* (head) of the well-known rabbinical academy in Sura, Babylonia.

Saadyah was also a pioneer in Hebrew philology. He translated the Bible into Arabic, and his commentaries on it laid the foundation for a scientific interpretation of the Bible. Much of his extensive literary output focused on polemics against the Karaites, a Jewish sect that accepted the biblical text (*kara* in Aramaic) alone and rejected all Rabbinic interpretation of oral law. Saadyah's entire system of philosophy can be found in his book *Beliefs and Opinions*. His doctrine concerning the relationship between reason and revelation—which was accepted by most subsequent Jewish philosophers—provided the methodological foundation for his religious philosophy. For him, religious truth, a distinct form of truth, is found in revelation. Reason provides the common foundation for all religions. For Saadyah, only Judaism is the work of God; all other religions were developed by humankind and therefore falsely claim divine origin.

GLEANINGS

Freedom to Escape

Life is inescapably filled with meaning. That is because the whole thing is prearranged. We have no more freedom than an oak tree. That is, we are free to be who we are or free to pretend that we are someone else. But we are not free to be someone else.

And this is the meaning of meaning: Being connected with something that is itself connected with something. Being part of a constellation of parts that is itself part of an even greater scheme. Or, in other words, that the notion of parts is in truth, a convenience we perpetuate so as to permit us not having to fathom the consequences of our most trivial acts. Nothing is entirely separate. No one acts with caprice. The Holy One is always involved.

Freedom, in the way most people use the word, is only an excuse to insist on moral culpability which is only an excuse to pretend that the social good we do is from fear of punishment—instead of saying that we do everything we do because we want to. Which is the same as saying that we have no alternative. No alternative except one. We are free to be aware of the significance of each moment. To understand our destiny. Or to avoid it.

"All is in the hands of Heaven" save the fear of Heaven (Berachot 33b). To fear Heaven is to search for the holy intention that might be realized by our every act or discerned everywhere round about us.

Lawrence Kushner, Honey from the Rock: Visions of Jewish Mystical Renewal
(Woodstock, VT: Jewish Lights Publishing, 1990), 58–59

A Document of Change

Jonah is the great document of human change, and as such is given a central place in the Yom Kippur liturgy. As the day draws to a close and we feel near despair at our failure to achieve transformation, Jonah and the people of Nineveh are brought forth to tell us not to lose heart, that change is always possible, that all human lives can be given new beginnings.

The book documents two changes: that of the Ninevites and that of the prophet himself. The repentance of the Ninevites is of the more conventional kind: Warned of their destruction, they take the message to heart and return to God. But the book's deeper message may be the tale of Jonah himself, the hardened cynic who does not believe that their repentance will be real. He flees his task because he does not believe in people, does not believe that there will be an authentic change of heart. He is left without compassion, embittered by the ease with which God has let His sinners off the hook. Only the incident of the gourd, a simple thing of nature that he has come to love, reminds him that God's mercies know no bounds, and tells us that every human heart will sooner or later find that which calls it forth to open.

Arthur Green, in *The Jewish Holidays: A Guide and Commentary*, ed. Michael Strassfeld
(New York: Harper & Row, 1985), 116–17

Reasons for Repentance

Why do our mistakes, our transgressions of the *mitzvot*, call us to repentance and stir us to seek forgiveness?

A most compelling reason is that if we believe that the commandments came directly from God, that they are God's will for us, then as children of God, we must obey His law. The power of God calls us to follow His rules, and if we obey them, to say, "I'm sorry."

Beyond that, the Torah repeats, time and time again, the conditional nature of the covenant. "*If* you obey My commandments and observe My *mitzvot, then*, I will reward you. *But, if* you disobey and transgress My *mitzvot, then* I will bring punishment upon you" (see, especially, Leviticus 26).

The people of biblical times truly believed that *if* they followed God's law, *then* the rains would come, the crops would grow. But *if* they disobeyed God's law, *then* they would be thirsty and hungry (see, especially, Deuteronomy 11:13 ff). The prophets take up where the Torah leaves off, foretelling severe punishment for the people and for the Jewish nation if God's commands are not fulfilled, linking transgression of *mitzvot* to the eventual conquering of the Land of Israel, the destruction of the Holy Temple and the exile of the people.

To many of us, the *if-then* covenant may seem fallacious: We see little evidence of a causal relationship between human behavior and whether or not the rains fall.

Yet we cannot deny that there is a connection between how we act—whether or not we obey God's law—and what ultimately happens to the world in which we live.

God doesn't really have to intervene, because we bring reward or punishment upon ourselves: Every action causes a reaction; every act has a consequence; every word ripples through time. Everything we do and say affects those around us— our jobs or businesses, our communities, our neighborhoods, our organizations, our spouses, our children, our relatives, our friends. Everything we do and say determines whether things will be good or bad, easy or hard, loving or alienating.

To be sure, there is random happenstance; we cannot control the actions of others who choose to do evil rather than good; we cannot tame all of the forces of nature. But we can have an effect on our small worlds: our offices, our homes, our marriages, our relationships. And since the whole world is ultimately made up of individual human beings—just like you and me—then we can and ultimately do have an effect on how our whole world works.

Wayne Dosick, Living Judaism: The Complete Guide to Jewish Belief, Tradition, and Practice
(New York: HarperSanFrancisco, 1995), 145

To Grow in Soul

Judaism insists we can overcome the past. The Hebrew word *teshuva* means both "turning" and "answer." Turning from sins we have committed, we answer the persistent question of each soul: How can I change and unburden myself of my past?

Teshuva means acknowledging one's sin, regretting it, seeking to repair it, and re-solving not to repeat it. We change the past by making our sins markers to a new place. Before we had "turned," our sins were stones on our souls. Now, having done *teshuva*, our transgressions become the catalyst for a renewed self. Each sin becomes a stepping-stone. The past is recast, because it leads to a new place.

To be a faithful Jew means to scour one's soul, seeking to force oneself deeper. *Teshuva* is a hard test; we must not only examine ourselves, we must ask forgiveness from those whom we have hurt. Without confronting those who have suffered by our sins, we cannot do *teshuva*. Repentance must move through us and into the hurt eyes of another human being. We may feel kind and good, but only interchange with others will show if our self-perception is accurate. Without the courage for that confrontation, *teshuva* remains incomplete.

"Though your sins be scarlet, they shall become white as snow" promises the prophet Isaiah (1:18). Sins themselves become transformed when they change our lives. *Teshuva* teaches how to integrate even our sins into the work of art each of us seeks to create from life.

We seek *teshuva* because *in the Jewish tradition the aim of life is to grow in soul*. That is why an old rabbinic saying asserts that a repentant sinner stands upon a height that not even the greatest *tzaddik* (righteous person) can reach.

David J. Wolpe, Why Be Jewish? (New York: Henry Holt, 1995), 24–25

CHAPTER TWO

ב:א וַיְמַן יְהֹוָה דָּג גָּדוֹל לִבְלֹעַ אֶת־יוֹנָה וַיְהִי יוֹנָה בִּמְעֵי הַדָּג שְׁלֹשָׁה
יָמִים וּשְׁלֹשָׁה לֵילוֹת:

2:1 *ADONAI* ARRANGED FOR A GREAT FISH TO SWALLOW
JONAH, AND JONAH WAS IN THE BELLY OF THAT FISH
FOR THREE DAYS AND THREE NIGHTS.

This is a familiar verse to many people, who may be surprised to note that the Hebrew does not specify the kind of fish and certainly does not suggest—as some others
have—that it is a whale that swallows Jonah. The author uses the root *m-n-h* in what
is called the *pi·eil* form to indicate the sense of "appoint, send, or arrange" (Koehler-
Baumgartner, *Lexicon*, p. 599). We have chosen to render the Hebrew as "arrange
for." The *Targum* translates *vay'man* as *zamein* (appoint). However it is translated, the
idea is conveyed that Jonah is swallowed because of God's intervention.

Rashi tells us that the fish is male. However, since Jonah is comfortable within, he
does not think of praying while inside it, and God orders the fish to vomit him out.
Subsequently, a pregnant female fish swallows Jonah. At that point, Jonah, crowded
by all the fish eggs, is forced to pray. Rashi comes to this conclusion based on the
word for "the fish" (*hadag*). In this verse, the word is masculine, so he reads it as "the
male fish." However, in the following verse, the author uses *hadagah*, a feminine
form. Rashi thus reasons that there must be a second, female fish.

Ibn Ezra finds it necessary to point out that no one could survive inside a fish for an
hour. Jonah's survival in the belly of the fish for three days and three nights is therefore
a miracle caused by God.

Redak tells us that the very moment that Jonah is cast overboard, the fish swallows
him so that Jonah will not sink to the depths of the sea. He bases this idea on a statement of Rabbi Tarfon, who says that the fish had been appointed to the task during

the first six days of Creation (*Pirkei D'Rabbi Eliezer* 10). This reading implies that all of Jonah's actions have been anticipated by God ahead of time. The constant role of God continues to be emphasized in this tale, rather than Jonah's choice in turning back to God's will.

ב:ב וַיִּתְפַּלֵּל יוֹנָה אֶל־יְהֹוָה אֱלֹהָיו מִמְּעֵי הַדָּגָה:

2:2 NOW JONAH PRAYED TO *ADONAI*, HIS GOD, FROM THE
     BELLY OF THE FISH.

It is not surprising that Jonah prays to God. Who wouldn't pray upon being cast into the water—even when not swallowed by some sort of big fish? Prayer is a natural response at a time of fear or crisis. In order to avoid anthropomorphism, the *Targum* has Jonah pray "before *Adonai*" rather than "to *Adonai*." This is a subtle distinction, but the *Targum* uses this difference to move the reader away from the assumption that God acts similarly to humans. The difference in meaning could be understood as praying in a general sense "in the presence of God," versus praying to a specific thing or place. But the *Targum* appears to be unconcerned that Jonah is able to enter a fish and exit it without any apparent harm. Ibn Ezra suggests that many commentators misread the text and conclude that Jonah prays from inside the fish. For Ibn Ezra, the inclusion of the word "from" in the verse indicates that Jonah prays only after he leaves the fish. For Redak, it is a miracle that Jonah survives for three days inside of a fish—under water. Since he is able to pray, it means that his mind was not ill-effected by his consumption. Redak reasons that this too is a miracle. This story clearly troubles the Rabbis, and the only way they can feel comfortable is to turn the event into a miracle. The liturgy on Yom Kippur features similar kinds of divine intervention.

ב:ג וַיֹּאמֶר קָרָאתִי מִצָּרָה לִי אֶל־יְהוָה וַיַּעֲנֵנִי מִבֶּטֶן שְׁאוֹל שִׁוַּעְתִּי
שָׁמַעְתָּ קוֹלִי:

**2:3 HE SAID, "IN MY NEED, I CALLED TO *ADONAI* AND
GOD ANSWERED ME. FROM THE BELLY OF SHEOL, I
CRIED OUT, AND YOU HEARD MY VOICE.**

This verse is a classic statement of faith, regardless of the context: "I called out to God
from the depths of my despair. God responded to my prayers and lifted me up." It is
precisely what we want to know on Yom Kippur—we want to be assured that God
will hear and respond to our prayers.

The word Sheol, which we understand here as a proper noun, generally means
"wasteland, void, underworld" (cf. Koehler-Baumgartner, p. 1,369), that is, some-
place on land or under it. Here it refers to the depths of the sea. The *Targum* translates the word as *arit t'homah* (the bottom of the deep). Rashi explains that "belly" is
a reference to the belly of the fish. It seemed like a pit, like Sheol, to Jonah. Ibn Ezra
also understands the term as a deep place, the opposite of the heavens. The use of
these words emphasizes how low Jonah has sunk, similar to how one must sometimes
hit bottom before being able to turn one's life around. Sometimes it takes reaching
this level of despair before we are able to raise ourselves up to the task at hand.

Redak explains that Jonah's statement, "God answered me," comes after he realizes that he would safely leave the belly of the fish. Until that time he would not have
sufficient faith to make such a statement.

ב:ד וַתַּשְׁלִיכֵנִי מְצוּלָה בִּלְבַב יַמִּים וְנָהָר יְסֹבְבֵנִי כָּל־מִשְׁבָּרֶיךָ וְגַלֶּיךָ
עָלַי עָבָרוּ:

**2:4 "YOU THREW ME INTO THE DEEP, INTO THE HEART OF
THE SEAS. THE CURRENT SURROUNDED ME. ALL THE
BREAKERS AND THE WAVES PASSED OVER ME.**

This verse continues Jonah's description of what has taken place. In referring to the
bodies of water, note that the writer moves from singular noun to plural noun,
providing a sense of smallness in contrast to the great vastness of the sea.

Ibn Ezra comments that the plural "seas" may indicate a thematic connection between the Re(e)d Sea and the Mediterranean. However, it might be said that since Ibn Ezra knows that there is a geographic connection between these two bodies, he saw such a connection in this verse. Redak expands the connection and explains that *nahar* (current) is the proper name for the Tigris, placing Jonah in a geographic context. Then he explains that "breakers" are due to storms out at sea. The connection of these seas to each other also helps to emphasize God's role in the order of the universe—all the waters are connected and all are under God's rule. The commentators have to try to explain such a rough storm considering that Jonah hasn't yet made it out to the open sea.

ב:ה וַאֲנִי אָמַרְתִּי נִגְרַשְׁתִּי מִנֶּגֶד עֵינֶיךָ אַךְ אוֹסִיף לְהַבִּיט אֶל־הֵיכַל קָדְשֶׁךָ:

2:5 "I HAD SAID THAT I WAS THRUST AWAY FROM YOUR SIGHT. YET, I WILL AGAIN LOOK UPON YOUR HOLY TEMPLE.

The last clause in this verse presents us with two challenges. First, the introduction of the Temple and the Temple cult (also in 2:8, 2:10) seems contrived and out of context. Second, the final clause of this verse may be read either as a statement or as a question. It is unclear which is intended. But what is clear is that the author places words of optimism in Jonah's mouth. While Jonah may feel distanced from and by God, he will eventually return to a positive relationship with the Divine.

Rashi reads the first clause as a statement by Jonah. When he was cast into the sea, he thought that he was about to die and was thus driven from God's protective sight. He reads the second clause also as a statement made by Jonah. In this statement, Jonah declares that since God preserved him through this dangerous time, he will be able to again see the Temple.

Redak's explanation of the verse is rather sophisticated. For him, when Jonah states, "I had said," what he means is "I thought," indicating his fear of being disconnected from the God he had earlier tried to run from. Being "thrust away from God's sight" means "thrust away from God's providence." Having experienced the miracle of surviving in the belly of the fish, Jonah now knows that he will again look at the Temple—the place of prophecy and divine providence. He knows too that God will bring him back even if he were to attempt to flee. This interpretation is predicated on the idea that Jonah has reached a new point in his relationship with God. He accepts his role as a prophet. He understands that no matter how far he may have strayed, God will always welcome him back.

ב:ו אֲפָפוּנִי מַיִם עַד־נֶפֶשׁ תְּהוֹם יְסֹבְבֵנִי סוּף חָבוּשׁ לְרֹאשִׁי:

2:6 "THE WATERS OVERWHELMED ME. THE DEPTHS SURROUNDED ME. THE WEEDS TWISTED AROUND MY HEAD.

In this verse, the author attempts to offer the reader insight into Jonah's experience in the sea. His ordeal is made more dramatic through the use of illustrative details. In addition to the descriptive words, this verse contains difficult phrasing. The phrase *ad nefesh* (literally, "unto the soul"), translated here as "overwhelmed me," is hard to translate idiomatically. The *Targum* understands this phrase as *ad mota* (until death). Ibn Ezra reads it as "until I had almost died," as does Redak. Whatever the exact translation, these words give voice to Jonah's sense of desperation. It is ironic that what saved Jonah, according to Redak, is being swallowed by the fish. Otherwise, he would not have been able to survive in the water. Our future never looks as precious as it does when threatened, and near-death experiences often force us to change direction. Jonah's experience of being swallowed enables him to reconsider his direction and make different choices.

Following the *Targum*'s understanding of the word *suf* (literally, "weeds"), a reference to *yama d'suf*—the Sea of Reeds or the Re(e)d Sea—Rashi offers an interesting interpretation of the last clause. Jonah is afforded a vision of how the Israelites passed through the Re(e)d Sea on their way to freedom. According to Rashi, the eyes of the fish serve as underwater viewing windows.

Redak reminds us that *suf* can describe either weeds or reeds, depending on where they grow. Since some grew at the shore, at the end *(sof)* of the land, they were called *suf*. Since Jonah is surrounded by a fish, his description is apt. Nonetheless, we may feel the same way when we are overwhelmed by the events and stresses in our lives.

בּ:ז לְקִצְבֵי הָרִים יָרַדְתִּי הָאָרֶץ בְּרִחֶיהָ בַעֲדִי לְעוֹלָם וַתַּעַל מִשַּׁחַת
חַיַּי יְהוָה אֱלֹהָי:

2:7 "DOWN I WENT TO THE BASE OF THE MOUNTAINS.
THE BARS OF THE EARTH WOULD ALWAYS BE OVER ME.
YET, *ADONAI*, MY GOD, YOU BROUGHT ME UP FROM
THE PIT.

In this verse, the author suggests that not only has Jonah been cast to the depth of the sea, he has also been brought down to the subterranean land beneath the sea. He has been brought to a primordial state. Ibn Ezra explains the word *l'kitzvei* (to the bases), from the root *k-tz-v* (cut, hew), as an indication of both the way that the mountains were formed and the depth to which Jonah has sunk.

Although the Hebrew uses the term *chayai* (literally, "my life"), translating this verse into American English requires the use of "me" instead. Rashi reads this verse in connection to 2:5. Whereas Jonah feared that he would always be kept from God's presence, he learns that God will protect him. Rashi understands Jonah's experience as a journey through the underworld to *Geihinom*. Redak understands Jonah's journey as a descent into the bedrock of the sea. But like Rashi, he too reads something foreboding in the verse, taking *mishachat* (the pit) to mean "the grave." For both of these commentators, Jonah's experience below the sea is like a taste of what life would be if he truly could separate himself from God. Jonah describes what it might feel like if forced to live a life divorced from a relationship with God, a suffocating life of darkness and debasement.

בּ:ח בְּהִתְעַטֵּף עָלַי נַפְשִׁי אֶת־יְהוָה זָכָרְתִּי וַתָּבוֹא אֵלֶיךָ תְּפִלָּתִי אֶל־
הֵיכַל קָדְשֶׁךָ:

2:8 "JUST AS MY LIFE WAS ABOUT TO SLIP AWAY FROM ME,
I REMEMBERED *ADONAI*. MY PRAYER REACHED YOUR
HOLY TEMPLE.

With these words, Jonah's faith is affirmed as someone who is focused on the Temple cult; he sees God's place on earth and the place from which God answers human prayers as the Temple. While this may seem limiting, it is no different from our notion that the synagogue is a sacred place where most of our formal prayers are offered. That is why we go to the synagogue on Yom Kippur and read the story of Jonah.

According to Koehler-Baumgartner (p. 814), the root *ayin-tet-fei* means "to be weak, without strength." Thus, the form of the verb used in this verse, *hitateif*, would mean "to feel weak." A literal translation of the first clause of the verse would be "when my soul felt weak upon me." Since Jonah seems to be trying to say that he remembered God as he came close to death and that he was delivered as a result of his prayers, we have translated the beginning of the verse as "just as my life was about to slip away from me." This translation allows for the commonly accepted understanding of *nafshi* as "my life."

In an attempt to avoid anthropomorphism once again, the *Targum* posits Jonah remembering *pulchana d'Adonai* (the service of *Adonai*) rather than simply *Adonai*. Additionally, the Targum has Jonah's prayer coming *l'kodomach* (before You). In explaining *hitateif*, Rashi refers readers to the use of the verb in Lamentations 2:12, where the context suggests "languished." In explaining the same word, Ibn Ezra offers a reminder that the simple form of the word is found in Psalm 102:1, where the context suggests "faints."

Redak teaches us that the language of the verse reflects the life-threatening difficulty in which Jonah finds himself. Tossed into the sea and consumed by a fish, Jonah thinks that he is doomed to die. Thus, he is motivated to pray. When he realizes that he is still alive, albeit in the belly of the fish, Jonah understands that his prayers have been answered. Perhaps Redak is suggesting that while we should not wait until we are near death to pray, when we open our eyes to our surroundings, we may find that our prayers have indeed been answered. Redak also suggests that "Your holy Temple" is a reference to the heavens (which, according to the understanding of the Rabbis, is a mirror image of all of Jerusalem) rather than the earthly Jerusalem where the ancient Temple stood.

בּ:ט מְשַׁמְּרִים הַבְלֵי־שָׁוְא חַסְדָּם יַעֲזֹבוּ:

2:9 "THOSE WHO MAINTAIN FALSE IDOLS FORSAKE THEIR LOYALTY.

Not only is this verse difficult to translate and understand, it also appears to be out of place. The verse seems to refer to the sailors on whose boat Jonah sailed. When their prayers to their own gods fail, they turn to the God of Jonah. While there are other forms of the root *sh-m-r* (keep, guard) that occur throughout the Bible, this particular form of the word (known as the *pi-eil* form), *m'sham'rim*, appears only here. Since this form can imply a sense of frequency, it is translated here as "maintain." The words *havlei shav* can have numerous meanings. *Hevel* means "a vapor, something evanescent," as in the well-known phrase from *Kohelet* often translated as "vanity of vanities, all is vanity" (Ecclesiastes 1:2). *Shav* means "in vain, uselessly," as in the commandment against swearing falsely (Deuteronomy 5:11). The latter two words and the root *sh-m-r* appear in the simplest sense of the verb, as found in the phrase *hashom'rim havlei shav* (Psalms 31:7). The second clause of the verse from Psalms, "But I trust in *Adonai*," suggests that the three words should be translated as "who keep false idols." Hence, we have translated these words as "who maintain false idols."

The last two words of the verse present their own challenges. *Chasdam* is derived from *chesed*, "mercy." According to Koehler-Baumgartner (pp. 336–337), *chasdam* has the obvious meaning of "steadfast love, loyalty, faithfulness," that is, "their steadfast love, their loyalty, their faithfulness." But it is difficult to relate *chasdam* to the verb *yaazovu* (they will forsake) unless *chasdam* is understood as that to which they ought to be loyal. For Ibn Ezra, the sailors were rejecting the love they had for their idols. Alternatively, *chasdam* is related to the use of *chesed* as "shame," as in Leviticus 20:17. If this sense of the word is applied, then the verse refers to the sailors rejecting the shame of their idolatry (cf. Koehler-Baumgartner, p. 336). We have chosen such a forced translation in order to maintain the text as it had been passed down, originally copied by the Masoretes in the first century C.E. The *Biblia Hebraica* (p. 931) proposes two possible emendations to the text to improve its comprehension: *machseihem* (their refuge) or *machmadam* (their delight). Both of these would make better sense when read with the verb *yaazovu*. However, the translation here reflects the idea that it is more important to struggle to make sense out of the text rather than to emend the text so that it make sense.

The *Targum* makes sense of the verse by adding *la k'amamaya* (not like the nations) to its translation of *m'sham'rim havlei shav* (who worship error) and translates the remainder of the verse as *mei-atar d'itotav l'hon inun yad'in* (since they don't know what is good for them).

Rashi takes the first clause as a reference to idolaters and understands *chasdam* in the second clause to refer to the benefit coming from God, whom they forsook. By linking this verse to the next, Rashi suggests that Jonah, unlike the idolaters, thanks God for all that he has received. Then Rashi adds the comment from *Pirkei D'Rabbi Eliezer* in which the author claims that the sailors ultimately all became Jews. According to his reading, the sailors simply witnessed the power of God and converted to Judaism as soon as it was possible to do so. Redak expands the citation from *Pirkei D'Rabbi Eliezer* and teaches that the sailors threw their idols into the sea once they reached Nineveh. After they disembarked in Jaffa, they went to Jerusalem, had themselves circumcised, and offered sacrifices in the Temple.

ב:י וַאֲנִי בְּקוֹל תּוֹדָה אֶזְבְּחָה־לָּךְ אֲשֶׁר נָדַרְתִּי אֲשַׁלֵּמָה יְשׁוּעָתָה
לַיהוָה:

2:10 "As for me, I will offer sacrifices to You with resounding thanks, and I will pay what I promised. Salvation is from *Adonai*."

Here Jonah expresses his gratitude to God for being saved. The rendering of his statement in English may sound foreign but is indeed a rather common notion. The *Targum* is troubled by the way the verse is structured and suggests that Jonah will be making sacrifices "before You" instead of "to You." Additionally, in the *Targum*, Jonah's salvation again comes "before *Adonai*" rather than "from *Adonai*." Ibn Ezra takes *vaani* (as for me) as a reference to the promise that Jonah made while still in the belly of the fish. Redak, however, disagrees with Ibn Ezra. He suggests that *vaani* means that Jonah made this statement later while he was in the midst of his community. This last notion is a rather powerful idea. Jonah is so taken by his personal redemption that he is willing to publicly share what he experienced with others, fully cognizant of God as the ultimate source of his deliverance. Perhaps there is a helpful lesson here about acknowledging God's role in our personal redemption.

ב:יא וַיֹּאמֶר יְהֹוָה לַדָּג וַיָּקֵא אֶת־יוֹנָה אֶל־הַיַּבָּשָׁה:

2:11 *Adonai* SPOKE TO THE FISH, AND IT VOMITED JONAH OUT ONTO DRY LAND.

This verse emphasizes the idea that God is responsible for the events in this book, regardless of how strange that may seem. The *Targum* translates this verse word for word, apparently unmoved by the implicit peculiarities of the language. Ibn Ezra reads the expression *"Adonai* spoke*"* as a metaphor: the fish, like Jonah, is compelled to fulfill the divine will. Ibn Ezra expresses concern about God's ability to speak to fish, but curiously he does not seem bothered by the idea of a fish swallowing a man whole and vomiting him out to safety. Similarly, Redak suggests that somehow God motivated the fish to cough Jonah up onto dry land.

Sheol

Sheol is best understood as the "abode of the dead." It is the underworld, which may also be a grave or a pit. It seems to be a physical place, a comfortless place beneath the earth—or at its center—where we all go to sleep following death. It is not a place of punishment; it is the place where all go following death. While it was never formally described, it appears to be well-known among the ancient Israelites. It is mentioned in numerous places in the Bible such as Genesis 37:35, where Jacob says, "I will go down to Sheol mourning my son [Joseph]." For other instances of the use of Sheol in different ways, see Genesis 42:38 and 44:31. Numbers 16:30 refers to the rebellion of Korach, and Deuteronomy 32:22 consists of Moses's last instructions to the people.

Geihinom

The Jewish version of "hell," *Geihinom* literally refers to a valley south of Jerusalem on one of the borders between the territories of Judah and Benjamin (cf. Joshua 15:8; 18:16). During the time of the monarchy, it was a site associated with a cult that burned children. Jeremiah condemned the practice. In the Rabbinic period, the name is used to refer to the place of torment reserved for the wicked after death. It stands in contra-distinction to *Gan Eden*, the "Garden of Eden," which, in Rabbinic literature, became known as the place of reward for the righteous. In the Bible, these two names never connote the abode of souls after death. Yet in Rabbinic literature, such references abound: in BT *P'sachim* 54a, *Geihinom* and *Gan Eden* are said to have existed even before the world was created; the midrash to Psalm 50:12 describes *Geihinom* as being at the left hand of God and *Gan Eden* at God's right.

Masoretic Text

Jewish scribes working from 500 to 1000 C.F. were known as the Masoretes. They meticulously copied the Scriptures and preserved them. The work of the Masoretes produced the Masoretic text of the Bible (i.e., the current Hebrew text). They also set the musical notes for reading known in Yiddish as *trope* and in Hebrew as *taamei hamikra*.

GLEANINGS

Repentance

"What is repentance? The One who knows all that is hidden will testify that the individual will never again repeat this sin." [Maimonides, *Mishneh Torah, Hilchot Teshuvah* 2:2].

How can God testify that once we have repented we will not commit a particular transgression again? We might argue that all is foreseen to God, therefore God knows what will happen. Other people will argue that the only real repentance comes at death and that once you die, you can, of course, no longer transgress on earth. Or so we think. Still others might say that since most of our life is lived in routine, we can follow people on their daily routines and discern whether they are tempted to transgress again. Those activities that are beyond daily routine may be beyond the possibility of transgression, since we have no prior experience with them.

I like to think of Maimonides' insight this way: God can peer into the soul of the individual and make a determination about our proclivity to sin even when we think we cannot do so on our own. This is accomplished through the light of Divine illumination. When we make use of this Light, we can find the recesses of self. Then we can more fully know the self.

Kerry M. Olitzky, "Repentance with a Warranty," in Kerry M. Olitzky and Lori Forman,
Sacred Intentions: Daily Inspiration to Strengthen the Spirit, Based on Jewish Wisdom
(Woodstock, VT: Jewish Lights Publishing, 1999), 266

Why Pray?

Thinking is prologue to prayer. For prayer is based on knowledge of what is real. To understand what is real is essential for the realization of the ideal. In the Jewish tradition, one is not to pray when intoxicated or confused. The liturgical world of the sane and sober is not the prayer world of the disordered and inebriated. Prayer leads to decision. Prayer has consequences. To pray wisely, we must know something about what the world is really like. The intent of petition is grounded in the possibilities of the real world....

The covenant prayer is not modeled according to the relationship of king to servant, or master to servant, or shepherd to flock. Covenantal prayer is a two-sided relationship of co-creators and co-sanctifiers. I am not a passive recipient of an Other's will, judgment, and act. I understand myself as an essential and active partner with the Divine Other. Conventional prayer increases the potency of the Divine Thou, by raising the power and the responsibility of the human partner to answer prayer.

Harold M. Schulweis, *For Those Who Can't Believe: Overcoming the Obstacles to Faith*
(New York: HarperCollins, 1994), 34, 36–37

Collective Responsibility and Repentance

Collective repentance is the renewal of the world's spirit. It is the lifting up of that spirit, the recovery of the divine, the bringing on of spring after the winters of our life. History yearns for penitential acts much the way that seedlings try so hard to break forth from the ground every year. The energies of man, therefore, have to be placed in this direction, too. Not only to bring economic miracles, but to bring a true renewal of spirit, a renewal that cannot take place without repentance first.

Harlan J. Wechsler, *What's So Bad about Guilt? Learning to Live With It Since We Can't Live Without It*
(New York: Simon and Schuster, 1990), 193

What Does God Say to Humans?

The voice of God is like the voice of the sea; it is ever there, but may be heard only by those who listen for it. In the heat and turmoil of mid-day, as in the stillness of the night, the ocean speaks, the waves roll out their even beat, the waters hit the shore with liquid sound. But one who lives at the seaside may spend day after day in engrossed absorption with his affairs, and not once hear the voice of the sea. It is only when he is listening for it, it is only when he detaches himself from the complete attention to things that had rendered him deaf to the sea, that he hears its wondrous voice. So God speaks to us all the time, but we are too engrossed to listen, and therefore do not even know that He is speaking. But if we would *listen*, what wondrous things we would hear.

Tehilla Lichtenstein, "What Does God Say to Man?" in *Applied Judaism:
Selected Jewish Science Essays by Tehilla Lichtenstein*, ed. Doris Friedman
(New York: Society of Jewish Science, 1989), 70

Finding Ourselves Worthy of God's Love

The liturgy will speak repeatedly of our failings, our neglect of our duties, our hard-heartedness toward others. But if the words of the Day of Atonement are words of rebuke and failure, the "music" carries a very different message. The people in synagogue have not come to be told that they have done things that were wrong. They know that all too well. They have come to be assured that their misdeeds have not separated them from the love of God. They are not looking to be judged and condemned. They are looking to feel cleansed, to gain the confidence and the sense of forgiveness and acceptance that will enable them to begin the New Year without the burden of last year's failures.

There seems to be something in the human soul that causes us to think less of ourselves every time we do something wrong. It may be the result of parents who expected too much of us, or of teachers who took for granted what we did right and fastened instead on everything we got wrong. And maybe it is good for us to feel that way. It may make us more sensitive to what we do wrong and move us to repent and grow. But it may also lead to our setting unrealistically high standards for ourselves and for others.

Religion sets high standards for us and urges us to grow morally in our efforts to meet those standards. Religion tells us, "You could have done better; you can do better." But listen closely to that message. Those are words of encouragement, not condemnation. They are a compliment to our ability to grow, not a criticism of our tendency to make mistakes. We misunderstand the message of religion if we hear it as a message of criticism, even as we misunderstood our parents, thinking they were disappointed in us when what they were trying to do, however awkwardly and maybe unrealistically, was prevent our one day looking back and being disappointed in ourselves for not having done our best. Religion condemns wrongdoing. It takes us to task for lying and hurting people. But religion also tries to wash us clean of disappointment in ourselves, with the liberating message that God finds us worthy of His love.

Harold S. Kushner, *How Good Do We Have to Be? A New Understanding of Guilt and Forgiveness*
(New York: Little, Brown, 1996), 6–7

CHAPTER THREE

ג:א וַיְהִי דְבַר־יְהוָה אֶל־יוֹנָה שֵׁנִית לֵאמֹר:

3:1 Now the word of *Adonai* came to Jonah a second time:

After Jonah is saved from death by drowning and from being eaten alive by a fish, God calls Jonah to his prophetic mission once again—the very mission Jonah had sought to avoid. With this second call, Jonah feels compelled to respond and seems to do so more willingly. It is human nature for people to often fall back to their former behavior when things return to normal and their life is no longer threatened. However, repentance requires learning how to maintain the new direction in life. After Yom Kippur, it is easy to forget the impact of the experience. Reading Jonah late in the day of Yom Kippur helps us focus on what long-term changes we need to make in our lives in the days and weeks that will follow.

In its ongoing effort to avoid anthropomorphism, the *Targum* translates the beginning of the verse as *pitgam nevuah min kodam Adonai*—"the word of prophecy from before *Adonai*"—to Jonah. Ibn Ezra notes that *vay'hi* (literally, "it was")—which we have translated as "now"—is an indication of an event happening a second time. Redak reminds us of something that we need to be continually reminded of: God forgives penitent people, regardless of their place or people of origin (see 1:1).

37

ג:ב קוּם לֵךְ אֶל־נִינְוֵה הָעִיר הַגְּדוֹלָה וּקְרָא אֵלֶיהָ אֶת־הַקְּרִיאָה אֲשֶׁר
אָנֹכִי דֹּבֵר אֵלֶיךָ:

3:2 "GET UP AND GO TO THE GREAT CITY OF NINEVEH,
AND PROCLAIM THERE WHAT I AM ABOUT TO TELL
YOU."

Jonah is about to receive his direction from God. The author wants to make sure that the reader knows the source of Jonah's instructions. Though it might be assumed that the repetition of the words from 1:2 in the beginning of this verse are simply used here for emphasis and reflect the author's literary style, the commentators remind us that there is meaning in everything in sacred literature. Ibn Ezra understands *kum* (get up) as an indication that Jonah had not yet gone very far from Nineveh—an implicit way for Jonah to communicate that were God to send him, he would go. Redak understands the repetition of the words from a previous verse as evidence of God's impatience and irritation with Jonah. God must use the same words a second time to make sure Jonah will listen.

ג:ג וַיָּקָם יוֹנָה וַיֵּלֶךְ אֶל־נִינְוֵה כִּדְבַר יְהוָה וְנִינְוֵה הָיְתָה עִיר־גְּדוֹלָה
לֵאלֹהִים מַהֲלַךְ שְׁלֹשֶׁת יָמִים:

3:3 FOLLOWING THE WORD OF GOD, JONAH GOT UP AND
WENT TO NINEVEH. NINEVEH WAS SUCH AN ENOR-
MOUS CITY THAT IT TOOK THREE DAYS TO CROSS IT.

The author emphasizes that this time Jonah followed God's direction. Our translation omits a literal translation of *l'Elohim* (literally, "unto God") following the description of Nineveh as *ir g'dolah* (a great city). While it could be translated as "to God," it seems more like the term is used as a superlative. (See Koehler-Baumgartner, p. 53.) Redak agrees with this perspective and suggests that if you wanted to magnify something, then you would compare it to God, as in *har'rei Eil* (great mountains) in Psalm 36:7 or *shalhevet Yah* (a great flame) in Song of Songs 8:6.

Ibn Ezra explains that those who had been aboard the ship whose crew threw Jonah overboard continued on to Nineveh. Once they arrived, the sailors told their story to the people. As a result, the inhabitants were prepared to believe Jonah when he came to speak to them. He adds that the use of "three days" as a measurement relates to the outskirts of the city, the city itself, and then the outskirts again. Thus, Ibn Ezra claims that it is only one day's journey from one end to the other.

ג:ד וַיָּחֶל יוֹנָה לָבוֹא בָעִיר מַהֲלַךְ יוֹם אֶחָד וַיִּקְרָא וַיֹּאמַר עוֹד אַרְבָּעִים יוֹם וְנִינְוֵה נֶהְפָּכֶת:

3:4 ENTERING THE CITY, JONAH PROCLAIMED GOD'S WARNING AS SOON AS HE HAD GONE ONE DAY'S JOURNEY INTO THE CITY: "IN FORTY DAYS, THE CITY WILL BE OVERTURNED."

Jonah doesn't wait. He issues God's warning as soon as he arrives in the center of the city. Rashi draws attention to the use of the term *nehpachet* (changed, altered) rather than *necherevet* (destroyed). He contends that the Hebrew word has two meanings: one is bad; the other is good. That is, if the people of Nineveh continue to sin, they will be destroyed. If they repent, they will be saved. Ibn Ezra rejects outright Rashi's explanation of the Hebrew, arguing that it is not an interpretation of the text, citing Jeremiah 49:18 to suggest that "alter" cannot be for good and for bad without a context. Redak posits that the word *nehpachet* is used to remind readers of Sodom and Gomorrah (Genesis 19:29).

The number forty appears throughout the Bible. It is probably both a metaphor for a long period of time and a time period with special cultural meaning in the ancient world. The Flood in the story of Noah lasts forty days and nights (Genesis 7:12). Later in Genesis (50:2–3), the embalming of Jacob takes forty days. Exodus 34:28 has Moses tarrying on the top of Mount Sinai for forty days and forty nights. The Israelites spent forty years in the desert before Joshua led them into the Promised Land; as God explains to Moses in Numbers 14:34, one year for each day the twelve scouts spent in Canaan. And Deuteronomy 25:3 suggests that up to forty lashes may be given as a punishment. In each case, the use of forty emphasizes the length or intensity of the experience.

ג:ה וַיַּאֲמִינוּ אַנְשֵׁי נִינְוֵה בֵּאלֹהִים וַיִּקְרְאוּ־צוֹם וַיִּלְבְּשׁוּ שַׂקִּים מִגְּדוֹלָם
וְעַד־קְטַנָּם:

3:5 BELIEVING IN GOD, THE PEOPLE OF NINEVEH PRO-
CLAIMED A FAST. AND FROM THE GREATEST TO THE
SMALLEST, THEY ALL PUT ON SACKCLOTH.

It is amazing to think that the people of Nineveh responded to Jonah so quickly. Our
experiences with behavioral change might suggest otherwise. Ibn Ezra helps us to
understand by suggesting that the people believed ''in the word of God.'' They were
able to immediately accept Jonah and respond to his warning. Redak reminds us that
since, according to his interpretation, the sailors had arrived previously, the people
already anticipated Jonah's admonition. Thus, they put on sackcloth, fasted, and
repented even before the king issued an edict (which we learn about in verse 3:7).

ג:ו וַיִּגַּע הַדָּבָר אֶל־מֶלֶךְ נִינְוֵה וַיָּקָם מִכִּסְאוֹ וַיַּעֲבֵר אַדַּרְתּוֹ מֵעָלָיו
וַיְכַס שַׂק וַיֵּשֶׁב עַל־הָאֵפֶר:

3:6 WHEN THE WORD REACHED THE KING OF NINEVEH,
HE GOT UP FROM HIS THRONE, TOOK OFF HIS ROYAL
ROBE, COVERED HIMSELF WITH SACKCOTH, AND SAT IN
ASHES.

This verse continues the picture of spontaneous remorse and repentance. This kind of
response is generally not found among the people or rulers of Israel, who were stub-
born and did not quickly change their ways until disaster struck. The entire Book of
Leviticus is built on this assumption. The traditional understanding of the destruction
of Jerusalem and the exile of the people is that these events were a direct result of
their behavior. Reform Judaism rejected such an understanding of the destruction and
exile. Nonetheless our experience with human behavior is such that we know people
often make changes in their lives after the results of their behavior are manifest.
Consider those who make lifestyle changes after experiencing health difficulties rather
than taking preventive steps ahead of time.

The *Targum* translates *adarto* (literally, "his robe") as *l'vushei y'kareih* (garments of his glory) and is the basis of our translating the word as "royal robe." Ibn Ezra explains that the first part of the verse occurred before the king put on sackcloth. He notes that the word *vay'chas* (he covered) assumes an object, namely, his body.

ג:ז וַיַּזְעֵק וַיֹּאמֶר בְּנִינְוֵה מִטַּעַם הַמֶּלֶךְ וּגְדֹלָיו לֵאמֹר הָאָדָם וְהַבְּהֵמָה הַבָּקָר וְהַצֹּאן אַל־יִטְעֲמוּ מְאוּמָה אַל־יִרְעוּ וּמַיִם אַל־יִשְׁתּוּ:

3:7 HE ISSUED A PROCLAMATION THROUGHOUT NINEVEH: "BY THE DECREE OF THE KING AND THE NOBLES: LET NO HUMAN AND NO BEAST, NO FLOCKS AND NO HERDS TASTE ANYTHING. LET NONE GRAZE AND LET NONE DRINK WATER!

It is clear from the narrator's perspective that the king is taking the notion of repentance seriously and using the authority of his position to enforce it. Wanting to make sure that the posture of repentance is all-encompassing, he includes animals in the process. While the text literally says, "let every man," it is clear that the king's decree is to be understood to include everyone, including women. Therefore, we have used the word "human" in this verse and the next.

Since the basic meaning of *zaak* is "to cry out," Rashi explains the unfamiliar word *vayazeik* as "commanded and proclaimed" as a corollary to the use of "king and nobles." He uses both verbs to emphasize the difference between "kings and nobles." Only kings can command, whereas nobles make proclamations. Perhaps it was the role of nobles to advise the king in this matter, and the author is emphasizing their function. Ibn Ezra focuses on the word *mitaam* (by reason) as expressing the views and reflections of both the king and the nobles. The focus of Redak's comment is the practical question of how a proclamation works. He teaches that an announcer traveled throughout the city making a declaration in the king's name. The relationship between the king and the nobles in this verse provides an apt metaphor for Yom Kippur, in that we respond to God's directive for us to repent, as interpreted by the Rabbis through the liturgy.

ג:ח וְיִתְכַּסּוּ שַׂקִּים הָאָדָם וְהַבְּהֵמָה וְיִקְרְאוּ אֶל־אֱלֹהִים בְּחָזְקָה
וְיָשֻׁבוּ אִישׁ מִדַּרְכּוֹ הָרָעָה וּמִן־הֶחָמָס אֲשֶׁר בְּכַפֵּיהֶם:

3:8 "LET EVERY HUMAN AND EVERY BEAST BE COVERED
WITH SACKCLOTH, AND LET THEM CRY OUT LOUDLY
TO GOD. LET THEM ALL TURN FROM THEIR WICKED
WAY AND FROM WHAT THEY HAVE GAINED THROUGH
VIOLENCE.

This is a difficult text to translate, primarily due to differences between the Hebrew and English idioms. Nevertheless, it is clear that the king intends all of the inhabitants to repent. First, they must put on sackcloth. Then they must fast. And finally, they must cry out to God, presumably asking for atonement. The last clause of the verse, *umin hechamas asher b'chapeihem*, literally means "the violence which is in their hand." However, it would seem that what is intended is "what they have gained through violence," the violence that they personally caused or undertook with their own hands.

The *Targum* translates *v'yikr'u* (let them cry out) as *vitzalun kodam Adonai* (pray before *Adonai*). The sentiment of the author seems to be a combination of an unrestrained outpouring of emotion and prayer itself, which is usually seen as more specific and prescribed.

Rashi takes the same word (a masculine imperfect verb form) to indicate that the men of Nineveh locked all of the mothers in one place and all of the children in another place and said, "God, if you will not have compassion upon us, then we will not have compassion on the mothers and the children." It seems like a drastic action to make a point. Ibn Ezra uses the same word to refer to either an understanding person or to a person who is self-conscious about his sins. Redak tells us that "crying out" is an action that must be done wholeheartedly. For him, "wicked way" refers to one kind of sin and "what they have gained through violence" is a summary of all of the sins committed by the people of Nineveh.

ג:ט מִי־יוֹדֵעַ יָשׁוּב וְנִחַם הָאֱלֹהִים וְשָׁב מֵחֲרוֹן אַפּוֹ וְלֹא נֹאבֵד:

3:9 "WHO KNOWS? MAYBE GOD'S MIND WILL CHANGE AND
BE TURNED AWAY FROM ANGER SO THAT WE ARE NOT
DESTROYED."

This verse is a foreshadowing of God's eventual decision. Perhaps God never intended to destroy Nineveh, but wanted to give the people of Nineveh the opportunity to repent and change their ways. Because it is both commentary and translation, the *Targum* reads the verse in a very different manner. It takes the beginning of the verse as a reference to humans and leaves the remainder of the verse as a reference to God. It is uncomfortable with the possibility of the reader interpreting "Who knows?" as a challenge to God's omniscience. The first two words, *mi yodei-a* (who knows?), are translated as *man y'da d'it bidei chovin* ("who knows what transgressions one possesses"—literally, "are in one's hand"). The *Targum* translates the third word, *yashuv* (he will return), as *y'tuv* (let him repent). The next two words, *v'nicham haElohim* (and God will repent), are translated as *v'yitracheim alohi min kodam Adonai* (and *Adonai* will have compassion upon him). The next three words, *v'shav meicharon apo*, are translated as *vituv mit'kof rugzeih* (He will turn from the power of His anger). The last two words—perhaps the most important—are translated literally: "that we may not be destroyed." Thus, the *Targum* translation reads: "Who knows what transgressions one possesses? Let him repent and God will have compassion on him. God will turn from the power of divine anger so that we may not be destroyed."

Although Redak notes the view of the *Targum*, he interprets the phrase "Who knows?" as the king's own pondering—wondering whether God would rescind the decision to destroy the people once God sees that the people have repented. Redak also makes the suggestion that perhaps the first two words are not a question. Maybe they are a statement that suggests that the person who knows the way repentance works will repent, for then God will relent and not destroy the city. The commentator is concerned with the power of repentance to change God's decree over our lives. If it doesn't work, such reasoning implies, why bother? What do we personally gain that makes a difference to our lives?

ג:י וַיַּרְא הָאֱלֹהִים אֶת־מַעֲשֵׂיהֶם כִּי־שָׁבוּ מִדַּרְכָּם הָרָעָה וַיִּנָּחֶם
הָאֱלֹהִים עַל־הָרָעָה אֲשֶׁר־דִּבֶּר לַעֲשׂוֹת־לָהֶם וְלֹא עָשָׂה:

3:10 GOD, SEEING WHAT THEY HAD DONE IN TURNING
AWAY FROM THEIR EVIL BEHAVIOR, RELENTED DOING
THE PROMISED EVIL AGAINST THEM AND DID NOT
DO IT.

It is difficult to render the root *n-ch-m*. (The same challenge appears again in 4:2.) As Koehler-Baumgartner points out (pp. 688, 689), the root has the meaning "to be sorry, to regret, to console oneself." However, as its use in Exodus 13:17 indicates, the root often means "to change one's mind." It seems to have this meaning here. God has a change of mind and does not destroy the people. This suggests that God intended to do so initially. Thus, the repentance of the people has worked; it changes God's initial decision to destroy them, which God would have done had they not changed their ways. A second word makes the translation of this verse more difficult. The people of Nineveh did evil. Thus they would be punished by a similarly destructive act. But the Ninevites repent and God does not destroy them. The challenge in translation is in using an English idiom that reflects the sense of the Hebrew idiom. For this reason, *vayinachem...al haraah* is translated as "God...relented doing the evil." Similarly, Rashi explains the word *vayinachem* (He relented) as "reflecting on the promised evil, God turned from it." Perhaps God relents from the act of destruction because God knows it is an evil act. The very nature of God would suggest that God would not be capable of doing evil.

Sackcloth and Ashes

Most moderns think of wearing "sackcloth" as wrapping oneself in a burlap bag, perhaps with arm holes cut out. However, sackcloth was generally made of coarse, black goat hair. As its name indicates, this material was used for sacks rather than clothing. As a result, it was uncomfortable to wear and was not attractive. Sackcloth was customarily worn by mourners (who were focused on neither personal comfort nor vanity). This custom has been carried forward in some communities in the form of wearing black armbands (as opposed to black ribbons) as a sign of mourning. The wearing of sackcloth was also a sign of profound repentance and humility. Ashes were added as an additional symbol of self-abnegation. Thus, the people of Nineveh wore sackcloth and placed ashes on their faces as a sign of deep regret and an earnest desire to change their behaviors. The customs among Catholics regarding Ash Wednesday probably grew out of this originally Jewish custom.

GLEANINGS

T'shuvah *Action*

Teshuvah implies action. Just as you chose to do a wrongful act, so you can choose to right the wrong in the present and do good in the future. It is always within your power to return your steps to the right path.

The rabbis took this notion of turning very seriously. It is central to their understanding of human free will. Because you have the power to turn, to perfect yourself, you are never simply a creature of habit. You choose how you act moment to moment. Indeed, according to the rabbis, the power to turn from evil preceded the very creation of the world. Before evil existed, God had already established the power to turn from it and do good.

Teshuvah, however, is not just a matter of willpower. We all know how hard it is to do the right thing, even when we are clear as to what that is. Judaism teaches that all we have to do is make the first move; if we turn toward righteousness, the power of God will come to our aid and help us complete the process.

Rami M. Shapiro, *Minyan: Ten Principles for Living a Life of Integrity*
(New York: Bell Tower, 1997), 156

Divine Silence

The relationship between the prophet's own mind, education, and creative impulse, and the prophecy "given" has long been thrashed out by commentators. There have always been literalists, who believe the prophet to be merely a passive instrument into whose mouth God places the very words he or she is to speak. Others have long held the prophet to be an active participant in the process of revelation. Filled and consumed by the divine message, prophets put it into words using their own powers of articulation and the tools of the literary/religious tradition in which they stand. . . .

Postbiblical Judaism lives beyond the reach of current prophecy. God is still present and accessible in daily life and may be addressed through prayer. But God no longer speaks as happened in prophetic times. Divine silence is a mystery that we have learned to accept, despite an occasional outcry of protest. We study the prophets of old, endlessly re-interpret their words, and still feel morally challenged by them. We produce poets and writers who occasionally don the prophetic mantle, but we are as cautious of them as we are moved by their efforts. In the messianic future, whenever and whatever it will be, we are told that true prophecy will be reborn. Meanwhile, we can only live and witness the mystery of God's silence.

Arthur Green, *These Are the Words: A Vocabulary of Jewish Spiritual Life*
(Woodstock, VT: Jewish Lights Publishing, 1999), 165–166

Everything That We Do

Everything that happens to us, is us. There are so many times when we want to deny this, to blame others, to pretend it never happened, to distance ourselves from the ugliness we may have been a part of. There are other times when we cannot accept our success. We downplay our goodness, we slough off our accomplishments, we fail to take credit when it is due, we do not allow others to be grateful for what we have done. Both the negative and the positive, as well as all the moments in between—that is our life. And in order for us to be wholly and truly ourselves, we will need to take responsibility for it all.

Terry Bookman, *The Busy Soul: Ten-Minute Spiritual Workouts Drawn from Jewish Tradition*
(New York: Perigee, 1999), 143

Reward and Punishment

Hope for reward for the good that we do and fear of punishment for our misdeeds is the language in which we express the conflict between life and death in the human soul. Hope for reward embodies our desire to live without sin. Fear of punishment reflects our experience of the inevitable failure of that hope and our acceptance of the fact that such a failure has consequences. Reward and punishment are ancillary to the free will which defines our own mortality. Without reward and punishment, we must posit a world in which the transcendence of mortality is impossible. This would be a world without ultimate reward. Transcendence would not depend on our activities in this world and would be dispensed by an arbitrary God. Both of these possibilities run counter to the experience of God in the imagination of the people Israel.

Some in our tradition fear that human striving to imitate God is somehow debased if performed in anticipation of some kind of reward and punishment. But this misconstrues the Jewish experience of the divine. Logically, God's commandments must have consequences. And nothing indicates that these consequences will not be played out in this world to help us reduce moments-of-death in life, and in the next world so that we can appreciate life without death. To strive to reap the benefits of life without death and to strive to be chastened by punishment are among the highest yearnings available to us.

Ira F. Stone, *Seeking the Path to Life: Theological Meditations on God and the Nature of People, Love, Life and Death* (Woodstock, VT: Jewish Lights Publishing, 1992), 64

CHAPTER FOUR

ד:א וַיֵּרַע אֶל־יוֹנָה רָעָה גְדוֹלָה וַיִּחַר לוֹ:

4:1 BUT ALL OF THIS MADE JONAH VERY UNHAPPY AND
ANGRY.

Ironically, Jonah is upset because God relented. He wanted Nineveh to be punished.
No one likes to be made a fool. And as Jonah hadn't wanted to go on this mission in
the first place, he feels especially foolish. Rashi imagines Jonah thinking to himself,
"Now the nations of the world will think that I am a false prophet." As Redak points
out, a close reading of the text reveals the forty days had not passed yet. So the reader
is forced to ask: How does Jonah know that God relented and did not punish the
people? As indicated earlier, the specific number of days most likely does not matter,
since forty days simply represents a long time. However, Redak argues that God
informed Jonah through the spirit of prophecy. In other words, God told Jonah that
they would not be destroyed.

ד:ב וַיִּתְפַּלֵּל אֶל־יְהוָה וַיֹּאמַר אָנָּה יְהוָה הֲלוֹא־זֶה דְבָרִי עַד־הֱיוֹתִי
עַל־אַדְמָתִי עַל־כֵּן קִדַּמְתִּי לִבְרֹחַ תַּרְשִׁישָׁה כִּי יָדַעְתִּי כִּי אַתָּה
אֵל־חַנּוּן וְרַחוּם אֶרֶךְ אַפַּיִם וְרַב־חֶסֶד וְנִחָם עַל־הָרָעָה:

4:2 JONAH PRAYED TO GOD, SAYING, "*ADONAI*, THIS IS
EXACTLY WHAT I THOUGHT WHILE I WAS STILL ON MY
OWN LAND. THAT IS WHY I RAN OFF TO TARSHISH
BEFOREHAND, FOR I KNEW THAT YOU ARE A COM-
PASSIONATE AND MERCIFUL GOD, SLOW TO ANGER,
FULL OF STEADFAST LOVE, RELENTING [RATHER THAN]
DOING EVIL.

49

The author places a magnificent theological statement about the nature of God in the mouth of Jonah. On Yom Kippur, as we reflect upon our deeds and on the year just past, it is important for us to hear that God does not seek to destroy us, that is, to end our lives. Rather, God wants us to repent and will be compassionate, as is God's nature.

While the Hebrew idioms in this verse make a smooth translation into English difficult, the sense of the verse is clear. Jonah speaks out to God, "Look, this is why I didn't want to prophesy in the first place. I knew that You wouldn't destroy the people once they repented." *Davar*, as in *d'vari*, can mean "word, thing, matter," but the context here suggests "thought." In this verse, the author describes what Jonah thought rather than what he said. Hence, we have translated *d'vari* (literally, "my word") as "what I thought." We discussed the difficulty of the root *n-ch-m* in 3:10, although it appeared there in a different form. Here we have the sense "He will continually relent."

In the *Targum*'s translation, Jonah begins his prayer with the phrase *kabeil ba-uti* (receive my plea). It is a phrase of contrition, the same stance taken by those in the synagogue on Yom Kippur. In Rashi's interpretation of the verse, Jonah's hesitation came from his fear that he would look like a liar to the people of Nineveh, since he knew that they would repent and be spared by God. Rashi reasons that the people of Nineveh needed to be able to believe Jonah if they were to be persuaded to change.

In an interesting spin on the verse, Redak's understanding of Jonah's action is much more altruistic. In connecting this verse with the one that follows, Redak understands Jonah to be afraid that were the people of Nineveh to repent, it would look bad for the Jewish people. This interpretation is based on the idea that the Jewish people don't repent easily or completely. In his reading, Jonah thus fled before the second communication from God in order to not show the Jews, by contrast, in a negative light.

ד:ג וְעַתָּה יְהֹוָה קַח־נָא אֶת־נַפְשִׁי מִמֶּנִּי כִּי טוֹב מוֹתִי מֵחַיָּי:

4:3 "NOW, *ADONAI*, TAKE MY LIFE FROM ME, FOR MY DEATH IS BETTER THAN MY LIFE."

Jonah is portrayed in this verse as a bitter, irascible person. He would rather die than see a pagan people, sworn enemies of Israel, repent. While his actions seem drastic, they are perhaps familiar. It is not unusual for people to be so intent on the punishment of others that they lose their own way and are disappointed when people change their ways for the better. Rather than serving as a role model of ideal behavior, Jonah is presented as a fallible human being, a figure to whom everyone can relate.

Ibn Ezra explains that Jonah speaks on behalf of Israel. He is afraid that the destruction that God promised would be directed toward Israel, who remains unrepentant. In agreement with Ibn Ezra's position, Redak links this verse to Moses's actions following the episode of the Golden Calf: "Now, if You will forgive their sin [well and good]; but if not, erase me from the record which You have written!" (Exodus 32:32).

ד:ד וַיֹּאמֶר יְהֹוָה הַהֵיטֵב חָרָה לָךְ:

4:4 *ADONAI* REPLIED, "ARE YOU BETTER OFF BEING SO ANGRY?"

It is easy to hear the parent in the voice of God being spoken to Jonah. Nevertheless, it is difficult to render the precise meaning of the verb *heiteiv*, from the root *y-t-v*, here preceded by the particle *ha* (used as an interrogative). The Koehler-Baumgartner *Lexicon* (p. 408) translates the word as "to do well to be [angry]." But such a translation does not quite fit the idiomatic use of English. The *Targum* translates it as *lachada* (very much, too much). The phrase *halachada t'keif lach* would thus read, "Is it too vehement for you?"

Reaching for the real sense of the verse rather than an exact translation, Ibn Ezra understands it as "Why is it so difficult for you?" Jonah is being asked to figure out why he is so distraught at what should be good news. Redak sees this verse as an introduction for the verses that follow, as if to say, "If you are so angry about this, then

I will show you another wonder.'' Again, the reader can hear the parental voice in a slightly different context: ''If you think that hurts, I will give you something to cry about.'' Jonah has not finished learning about how to appropriately care for others and to appreciate God's role in the universe.

ד:ה וַיֵּצֵא יוֹנָה מִן־הָעִיר וַיֵּשֶׁב מִקֶּדֶם לָעִיר וַיַּעַשׂ לוֹ שָׁם סֻכָּה וַיֵּשֶׁב תַּחְתֶּיהָ בַּצֵּל עַד אֲשֶׁר יִרְאֶה מַה־יִּהְיֶה בָּעִיר:

4:5 So JONAH LEFT THE CITY, SETTLED DOWN TO THE EAST OF IT, AND MADE HIMSELF A BOOTH. HE SAT THERE BENEATH ITS SHADE, WAITING TO SEE WHAT WOULD HAPPEN TO THE CITY.

In an image reminiscent of small, simple huts workers made to protect them from the sun during rest periods at harvest season and like the temporary booths that the Israelites made while traveling in the desert, Jonah gets himself out of the sun and away from the city. If it is to be destroyed, he doesn't want to be caught near it. There is a hint of a pun in the text, which the *Targum* picks up in its translation. It is the end of the city, as it is in danger of being destroyed. So Jonah goes to the physical *end* of the city. The *Targum* translates the verse literally until the last three words, *mah yihyeh ba-ir* (what would be with the city), and renders this as *ma y'hei v'sof karta* (what would be at the end of the city).

Ibn Ezra takes the verse as an indication of what happened before the forty days of impending doom had passed. Thus, he suggests that Jonah ''left,'' *vayeitzei*, is the same as *vayifga*, Jacob ''alighted,'' in Genesis 28:11 because both verses begin the same way. Redak posits that Jonah waited to see if the inhabitants of the city would remain committed to their posture of repentance. In his reading, Jonah is skeptical that their repentance was sincere or would be long-lasting.

ד:ו וַיְמַן יְהֹוָה־אֱלֹהִים קִיקָיוֹן וַיַּעַל מֵעַל לְיוֹנָה לִהְיוֹת צֵל עַל־רֹאשׁוֹ

לְהַצִּיל לוֹ מֵרָעָתוֹ וַיִּשְׂמַח יוֹנָה עַל־הַקִּיקָיוֹן שִׂמְחָה גְדוֹלָה:

4:6 NOW *ADONAI*, GOD, ARRANGED FOR A GOURD TO RISE
OVER JONAH AND SHADE HIS HEAD TO RESCUE HIM
FROM DISTRESS. JONAH WAS VERY HAPPY ABOUT THE
GOURD.

The author uses the same root *m-n-h* in the selection and direction of the gourd as he
did with the instruction to the fish (in 2:1) to swallow Jonah. The use of this verb
indicates divine actions that propel the story forward.

Rashi takes a practical view of the verse and points out that gourd plants—which
had many leaves—were often used for shade. Jonah is rescued by the gourd from the
heat of the sun, hence his pleasure in it. Ibn Ezra notes that although Spanish scholars
identify the *kikayon* as a gourd, we really don't know what kind of plant is actually
intended.

What puzzles Redak is the actual function of the gourd plant, especially if Jonah
was already sitting inside the hut that he had made. One possible explanation is that
Jonah made the booth from plant and tree cuttings. After sitting in it for forty days, the
foliage dried out and no longer provided him any shade. That's when God provided
the *kikayon* and instructed it to grow so that Jonah could learn from the amazing
experience God orchestrated.

ד:ז וַיְמַן הָאֱלֹהִים תּוֹלַעַת בַּעֲלוֹת הַשַּׁחַר לַמָּחֳרָת וַתַּךְ אֶת־הַקִּיקָיוֹן

וַיִּיבָשׁ:

4:7 THEN THE NEXT DAY AT DAWN, GOD ARRANGED FOR
A WORM, WHICH STRUCK THE GOURD SO THAT IT
WITHERED.

Jonah is paying the price for his attitude. God is directing the scene in an attempt to
manipulate Jonah. Anyone who questions whether God has a relationship with
everyday events may find such a process difficult to believe. The use of the word

"arranged" suggests that God is orchestrating the scene down to the last detail, having chosen a specific worm to do the deed. Ibn Ezra struggles with the timing of these events, suggesting that this occurred the day after Jonah rejoiced in the growth of the gourd plant. The timing is an issue because verses 2 and 8 describe actions that appear to be happening at the same time or very quickly one after another, or the various events are separated by a day, since they occur at dawn and at sunrise. In verse 10, the gourd is said to have grown and withered at night, yet 4:6 doesn't seem to indicate the same thing. Nevertheless, the events in 4:6 appear to be more logical. Ibn Ezra seeks to create a logical order of the events. Redak's commentary is a bit more technical. He suggests that the worm was directed to attack the gourd by splitting the base of the plant—which it did. This caused the plant to release its internal moisture and consequently wither.

ד:ח וַיְהִי כִּזְרֹחַ הַשֶּׁמֶשׁ וַיְמַן אֱלֹהִים רוּחַ קָדִים חֲרִישִׁית וַתַּךְ הַשֶּׁמֶשׁ עַל־רֹאשׁ יוֹנָה וַיִּתְעַלָּף וַיִּשְׁאַל אֶת־נַפְשׁוֹ לָמוּת וַיֹּאמֶר טוֹב מוֹתִי מֵחַיָּי:

4:8 AT SUNRISE, GOD APPOINTED A SCORCHING EAST WIND. THEN THE SUN BEAT DOWN ON JONAH'S HEAD SO THAT HE FELT FAINT. NOW HE WANTED TO DIE AND SAID, "I WOULD RATHER DIE THAN LIVE."

Jonah's troubles continue to multiply. After witnessing God's compassion for the people of Niveneh and having benefited himself from God's gift of the *kikayon*, now Jonah experiences hardship brought on by God. Whereas in 4:3 he expresses the desire to die because of emotional discomfort, preferring death to seeing the people of Nineveh repent and be saved, now he wants to die because of physical discomfort. Though this could be grounds for criticizing Jonah's egocentrism, anyone who has ever been exposed to the intensity of the sun, as described by the author, may understand Jonah's feelings. To emphasize the wind's intensity, the author uses the word *charishit* ("scorching," according to Koehler-Baumgartner, p. 353) to describe the uncommon quality of the east wind.

The *Targum* connects *charishit* with *cheiresh* (deaf). Thus, it translates the phrase as *ruach k'dumah sh'tikah* (a silent east wind), as if to emphasize its fierce quality. Rashi goes a little further and describes the wind as so hot that it is able to still other winds. Ibn Ezra tells us that the wind is so strong that its sound deafens all those who hear it. All of these are effects to describe the nature of the wind to the reader. If it weren't so severe, Jonah wouldn't be motivated to make such an exclamation. The commentators feel that they have to justify his emphasis.

ד:ט וַיֹּאמֶר אֱלֹהִים אֶל־יוֹנָה הַהֵיטֵב חָרָה־לְךָ עַל־הַקִּיקָיוֹן וַיֹּאמֶר הֵיטֵב חָרָה־לִי עַד־מָוֶת:

4:9 GOD SAID, "ARE YOU BETTER OFF BEING ANGRY AT THE GOURD?" JONAH ANSWERED, "BETTER? I AM SO ANGRY THAT I COULD DIE."

The author continues to expose the reader to Jonah's ill-tempered personality. He is unwilling to accept repentant sinners, hoping that they would continue with their evil ways and be destroyed as a result. Perhaps this is the author's view of prophets, in general, rather than of just Jonah. Ibn Ezra suggests that God provided the gourd as a possible way to defuse Jonah's anger, thinking perhaps that his anger would die down after the gourd died.

ד:י וַיֹּאמֶר יְהוָה אַתָּה חַסְתָּ עַל־הַקִּיקָיוֹן אֲשֶׁר לֹא־עָמַלְתָּ בּוֹ וְלֹא גִדַּלְתּוֹ שֶׁבִּן־לַיְלָה הָיָה וּבִן־לַיְלָה אָבָד:

4:10 *ADONAI* SAID, "YOU WERE UPSET ABOUT A GOURD FOR WHICH YOU DID NOT LABOR AND WHICH YOU DID NOT GROW, WHICH APPEARED ONE NIGHT AND DISAPPEARED THE NEXT.

Rashi explains that the uncommon *bin lailah* (one night) is used to indicate the unusual nature of a plant that grows so extensively in one night. Ibn Ezra is concerned that readers may think that God had to labor to grow the gourd (since Jonah did not have to do so). Thus, he suggests the author wrote it this way so that the least so-phisticated reader could understand the verse. Similarly, Redak calls our attention to the verse from the Talmud that reminds us, "The Torah speaks in the language of humans" (BT *Y'vamot* 71a; BT *Bava M'tzia* 31b). The Torah, and all biblical texts, at times resorts to simplistic images of God because of the limitations of human language and understanding.

Furthermore, Redak wants his readers to understand why God was so concerned about the people of Nineveh. He suggests that all creations reflect God's mag-nificence, and humans—regardless of who they are or where they live—reflect God in the highest form. Although he does not say so overtly, Redak anticipates the verse that follows.

ד:יא וַאֲנִי לֹא אָחוּס עַל־נִינְוֵה הָעִיר הַגְּדוֹלָה אֲשֶׁר יֶשׁ־בָּהּ הַרְבֵּה מִשְׁתֵּים־עֶשְׂרֵה רִבּוֹ אָדָם אֲשֶׁר לֹא־יָדַע בֵּין־יְמִינוֹ לִשְׂמֹאלוֹ וּבְהֵמָה רַבָּה:

4:11 "SHOULD I NOT BE UPSET ABOUT THE GREAT CITY OF NINEVEH IN WHICH THERE ARE MORE THAN TWELVE THOUSAND PEOPLE WHO CANNOT TELL THEIR RIGHT HAND FROM THEIR LEFT AND ALSO MANY ANIMALS?"

It is possible the entire Book of Jonah was prepared just for the sake of this verse. There is much for us to learn in it. The comments that God makes (through the words of the author) are profound and insightful. Most of the time our focus is on the inconsequential of the everyday, and we ignore matters of life and death. This verse reminds us that the spiritual life, in its deepest sense, is directed toward the preser-vation and enhancement of human life. Hence, it is appropriate that the statement comes at the very end of the book—though some will argue that the book is never really concluded, since the last words are in the form of a question.

It is not clear who the author refers to when using the phrase "cannot tell their right hand from their left." It could be understood as those who are so simple that they can't differentiate between good behavior and bad and thus don't deserve to be punished. Rashi suggests that it is the children of Niveneh. But then he goes on to say that the animals represent the adults. They are named as such because they do not recognize God as their Creator.

Ibn Ezra suggests that the population of the city might be larger and that twelve thousand refers only to those who are innocent. He uses Sodom and Gomorrah as examples, maintaining that the cities would not have been destroyed had there been a sufficient number of righteous people living in them.

Redak maintains that there were none to punish in the first place. "Those who did not know their right hand from their left" were children—those too young to sin— and the animals, who are incapable of sinning. The twelve thousand were those who had repented and therefore escaped punishment.

Coming as this does at the very end of the story of Jonah, this question leaves the reader with the challenge to think about others and not just focus on oneself. Chosen by the Rabbis to be read on Yom Kippur, this verse reminds the listener that after having spent a day on introspection and self-reflection, it will soon be time to turn back to the world and reengage in a positive way. This final verse in the story of Jonah is a call to achieve repentance and renewal through caring for others.

False Prophet

While the prophet was God's spokesperson, anyone could imitate the words of the prophet. As a result, it was difficult to determine who was really speaking for God and who was what came to be known as a "false prophet." Apparently, miracles were no proof, since the prophets of other gods were known to perform tricks. Obviously, the real test of a prophet was whether his or her predictions came true. This was a lot easier when the recording of what took place (written as the prophet's prophecy) happened after the event. But prophecy was not merely about predicting the future. It also served as instruction to the people. Since messages of doom and destruction were unpopular, only true prophets would offer such messages, since they were not interested in popular reaction to them as a result of delivering the message. The real prophet wanted to prevent impending doom and beseech God on the people's behalf.

GLEANINGS

How We Respond

No, Jonah had known all along that the Lord is compassionate toward all his creatures. He tells us in chapter 4, verse 2: "This was in fact my thinking when I was still in my land [at the beginning of the story]; for this reason I proceeded to flee to Tarshish: For I know that you are a God compassionate and kindly, patient and gracious, who is sorry for [doing] evil." Jonah understands God's nature well enough— but he disagrees with it! He has no compassion in him. He believes in strict, unmitigated justice. Whether Jonah becomes convinced of God's case at the end of the book is not the story's concern. The story ends without divulging Jonah's reaction because it is not so important how Jonah responds. It is crucial how we, the audience, respond. The ending of the tale is in our hands.

Edward Greenstein, in The Jewish Holidays: A Guide and Commentary, ed. Michael Strassfeld
(New York: Harper & Row, 1985), 117

The Nature of God

This is the primary reality of the universe. God is everywhere, and somehow we fail to get it. It was voiced by our patriarch Jacob as he awoke from his sleep and called out, "Surely God is in this place, and I, I did not know it!" (Genesis 28:16), and it has been voiced by every great spiritual leader, every spiritual path ever since. There is no place devoid of God. Jacob needed to go to sleep in order to wake up to that truth. Others have found it through prayer, meditation, unexpected encounters, nature, God's revelation, simple acts of loving kindness, study, even a bush that burned unconsumed in the desert. God is with us, always at our side, wherever we may happen to be. We cannot see or touch this God, but we can feel the presence of the Holy One whenever we invite Him/Her in.

Terry Bookman, The Busy Soul: Ten-Minute Spiritual Workouts Drawn from Jewish Tradition
(New York: Perigee, 1999), 128

We Are Human

When we do something wrong, because we are human and our choices are so complicated and temptations so strong, we don't lose our humanity. But we lose our integrity, our sense of wholeness, of being the same person all the time. We create a situation where a part of us, our good self, is at war with another part of us, our weak and selfish side. We lose the focus, the singleness of purpose, that enables us to do the things that matter to us. That is when we need the religious gift of forgiveness and atonement (making our split selves *at one*). But should we ever conclude that there is no point in trying to be good because we can never be good enough, that is when we lose everything. Being human can never mean being perfect, but it should always mean struggling to be as good as we can and never letting our failures be a reason for giving up the struggle.

Harold S. Kushner, *How Good Do We Have to Be? A New Understanding of Guilt and Forgiveness*
(Boston: Little, Brown, 1996), 174

A Sense of Responsibility for Our Lives

Teshuvah instills and affirms a sense of responsibility for our own lives. It is not an easy process. It may feel uncomfortable to examine the ways we have as individuals and communities made choices that did not support the expression and well-being of our own soul, of the souls of others and of the divine in this physical world. Sometimes we attempt to comfort ourselves and others by saying that our life circumstances or, for example, our dysfunctional families have made us who and what we are and that we really had no choice. It is true that all these external influences have impacted who we experience ourselves to be, but if we get stuck in blaming others and ourselves, we are not able to access our capacity to transcend the external world, to connect with the divine and to reclaim our power of choice. Through *teshuvah* we come in touch with our essence and with the inner strength to express ourselves.

Melinda Ribner, *New Age Judaism: Ancient Wisdom for the Modern World*
(Deerfield Beach, FL: Simcha Press, 2000), 107–8

From Justice to Mercy

Jews gather on the holiest day of their calendar each year to ask for forgiveness. They pray that God move from His Throne of Judgment and sit instead in a Seat of Mercy. It is a day of prayer, fasting and *teshuvah*, attempting to return to the proper path.

Underlying the liturgy of the day is the belief that God waits for us to find the right path. God is there to help us turn our lives around, to meet us halfway. Though God is a judge, God's main goal is not punitive. God's main goal is to help us return to the proper path. Mercy, rather than justice, is God's main attribute.

Still, most synagogues have the words "Know Before Whom You Stand" written on the synagogue ark that holds the Torah. We are being watched as we behave in this world. There is a proper path we ought to follow, and ultimately

God is our Judge.

Michael Gold, *The Ten Journeys of Life: Walking the Path of Abraham*
(Deerfield Beach, FL: Simcha Press, 2001), 229

Biographies

Terry Bookman is senior rabbi of Temple Beth Am in Miami, Florida. His most recent book is *God 101*. Widely published in a variety of religious journals, he is well-known for his online spiritual forum, through which he offers spiritual workouts and guidance to participants each day.

Wayne Dosick is the spiritual guide of the Elijah Minyan and adjunct professor of Jewish studies at the University of San Diego. He is the author of *Golden Rules*, *Dancing with God*, and *When Life Hurts*.

Rabbi Michael Gold serves as the spiritual leader of Temple Beth Torah in Tamarac, Florida. He has served congregations in Pittsburgh, Pennsylvania, and Upper Nyack, New York. Rabbi Gold is the author of *And Hannah Wept*, *Does God Belong in the Bedroom?*, and *God, Love, Sex and Family*.

Arthur Green is a rabbi and former president of the Reconstructionist Rabbinical College. He is currently rector of the newly established Rabbinical School at Hebrew College in Boston.

Edward Greenstein is former professor of Bible at the Jewish Theological Seminary and is currently on the faculty of Tel Aviv University.

Harold Kushner is rabbi emeritus of Temple Israel in Natick, Massachusetts, and author of the bestseller *When Bad Things Happen to Good People*.

Lawrence Kushner is the scholar-in-residence at Congregation Emanu-El in San Francisco. Most recently, he was rabbi-in-residence at Hebrew Union College–Jewish Institute of Religion, New York. Rabbi Kushner served as spiritual leader of Congregation Beth El of Sudbury, Massachusetts, for twenty-five years and is the author of numerous books and articles, including *God Was in This Place and I, i Did Not Know*.

Tehilla Lichtenstein founded the Society of Jewish Science with her husband, Rabbi Morris Lichtenstein, in 1922. Following his death, she continued his work and became the first woman to occupy a Jewish pulpit in America.

Melinda Ribner, C.S.W., is the founder and director of the Jewish Meditation Circle and author of *Everyday Kabbalah: A Practical Guide for Meditation, Healing and Personal Growth*. She has also taught at the New York Kollel, a project of Hebrew Union College–Jewish Institute of Religion.

Harold M. Schulweis is a rabbi and the spiritual leader of Congregation Valley Beth Shalom in Encino, California. He is also the founding chairman of the Jewish Foundation for Christian Rescuers and the author of several books, including *Approaches to the Philosophy of Religion*, *Evil and the Morality of God*, and *In God's Mirror*.

Rami M. Shapiro is former rabbi and storyteller of Temple Beth Or in Miami, Florida. He is an award-winning poet and essayist whose liturgical poems are used in prayer services throughout North America. He is the author of *Wisdom of the Jewish Sages: A Modern Reading of Pirke Avot*. Rabbi Shapiro was most recently the executive director of Metivta in Los Angeles, California.

Ira F. Stone is rabbi of Temple Beth Zion–Beth Israel in Philadelphia and adjunct lecturer of Jewish philosophy at the Jewish Theological Seminary of America.

Harlan Wechsler is rabbi of Congregation Or Zarua in New York City and visiting assistant professor at the Jewish Theological Seminary of America, where he teaches theology and ethics.

David J. Wolpe is rabbi of Sinai Congregation in Los Angeles and the author of numerous books, including *The Healer of Shattered Hearts: A Jewish View of God* and *In Speech and in Silence: The Jewish Quest for God*.